AI & Google S

Introduction: The Evolution of Onl
Retrieval

Chapter One: The Development of Google Search

Chapter Two: Utilising Google Search for Your Business

Chapter Three: Understanding AI

Chapter Four: Combining AI and Google Search

Chapter Five: AI and Content Marketing

Chapter Six: The Impact of Voice Search and Virtual
Assistants

Chapter Seven: AI and Search Engine Marketing (SEM)
Beyond Google

Chapter Eight: AI and Social Media Marketing

Chapter Nine: AI and Multilingual SEO

Chapter Ten: AI and Local SEO

Chapter Eleven: The Future

Chapter Twelve: Navigating the Ethical Concerns

Chapter Thirteen: Conclusion Harnessing the Power of AI

Introduction: The Evolution of Online Information Retrieval

The Internet has become an integral part of contemporary society. No one can argue the significance of Google Search, the world's largest search engine, in enabling and sustaining that integration. Google Search is used by billions of people worldwide every day to access the amounts of information which we would have been utterly lost without. With its profound scope and application, it can be argued that it is now essential for any individual to understand how to get the most out of Google Search as it is becoming increasingly more useful for carrying out tasks spanning from searching for peer-reviewed scientific documents to finding your new favourite local business. As a result, ensuring people are empowered with all the basics of navigating and leveraging this expansive database has become an ever-growing priority.

The ever-evolving technological landscape has brought us to a digital age wherein we heavily rely on Google searches. It has become deeply ingrained in our everyday lives, impacting our access to information and dictating many aspects of how we process and respond to data. As such, exploring the significance of its usage and what it implies for contemporary society is an important step towards understanding this technology's power and importance to our modern context. Considering its various implications for privacy, knowledge gathering, opportunity, innovation, and more sheds light on the need for developing informed perspectives when navigating this new terrain.

Google Search has had an incredible impact on how both individuals and businesses interact with technology. The sheer scope of its significance is staggering. By providing quick and easy search results, it has allowed information to be more easily accessed than ever before. For businesses, the implications of this are immense. They can use Google Search to market their services or products, increasing visibility and giving them a competitive edge. Businesses are able to expand their reach by harnessing the power of SEO (Search Engine Optimisation), allowing customers from all over the globe to discover them. Ultimately, Google Search has revolutionised how we find and share information, opening up endless opportunities for businesses of all sizes.

It has created a new platform for businesses to reach customers, providing instant access to any information at their fingertips. People now have the power to find and compare products with a few simple clicks, allowing businesses to expand their online presence and provide value through more targeted marketing. The shift away from traditional advertising into digital advertising has made it easier than ever for customers to get all of the information they need on a product with minimal effort. Google search's impact on society is profound; it has connected countless people worldwide and given them easy access to any information they need. Moreover, it has provided an invaluable tool for businesses, allowing them unprecedented insights into customer habits and preferences, ultimately taking their business goals further than ever before.

In recent years, the evolution of Google's Search capabilities has significantly impacted the way consumers purchase items online. Consumers are now turning to search engines to help with their buying decisions and access relevant product information quicker than ever before. With reflexive searches, it has become easier for users to access data specific to their needs and make better-informed purchasing choices. As a result, many companies have begun revamping their digital marketing and commerce strategies in order to meet these changes in consumer behaviour head-on. Google's technology is therefore playing an important role in driving this new digital buying process within businesses around the world.

The modern digital buying process is seen in the instant access of products and services on outlets such as smartphones and laptops - virtual stores now provide an equally optimised experience to physical ones. With simplified user interfaces adjusted for any unique customer journey, buyers can discover a vast inventory online without needing to step into a store. The purchase landscape is also changing with the option of functionality-rich sites enabling customers to avail of multiple payment methods, including instalments, custom billing, and easy returns. As this heightens simplicity with trustworthy options, many customers prefer the convenience offered with well-informed decisions at their fingertips instead of visiting actual shops. Ultimately, the digital buying space has not only helped reduce costs but provided users with the unprecedented choice to customise their searches and receive quality goods without ever leaving home.

With so much of the shopping experience now taking place online, understanding the digital buying process is essential. As soon as customers enter an e-commerce platform, they are met with an array of options that cater to their individual choices and needs. This can range from registering to the site or clicking a single buy button. Depending on the type of checkout option selected, customers may need to add payment or shipping information before the purchase is complete. To make this process even more accessible, consumers can opt for pre-stored payment preferences like one-click buying and online wallets. Once all these steps are through, buyers get access to their product or service quickly and securely for a seamless customer experience.

In today's digital age, utilising Google Search can be an instrumental tool for businesses to promote their services and reach potential customers. That is why this book aims to provide readers with an in-depth understanding of how best to leverage Google Search for business growth. Not only that, but this book will also explore the role of Artificial Intelligence (AI) in refining queries and increasing relevancy as well as comprehending natural language searches. By understanding how AI works within Google Search tools, readers will gain invaluable insight into how they can better optimise their own marketing strategies on Google's platform.

In this book, we will be examining the ways in which businesses can utilise the power of Google Search to enhance their operations. We will take an in-depth look at how Artificial Intelligence (AI) is changing the way Google Search operates and what businesses can do to ensure they are taking the best advantage of these developments in order to maximise their presence on the web. This book is for businesses and individuals seeking to understand not only what Google Search has to offer but also the impact that AI is having upon it so that they can rest assured that their web activities are as effective as possible.

Chapter One: The Development Of Google Search

Google Search, the world's most widely used search engine, began its journey as a research project by Larry Page and Sergey Brin, two Stanford University graduate students, in 1996. Originally named "Backrub," the search engine's primary innovation was using a new algorithm called PageRank, which assessed the relevance of websites by analysing the number and quality of links pointing to them. This approach allowed for more accurate search results than existing search engines, which primarily relied on the number of times a keyword appeared on a webpage.

In 1997, the project was renamed "Google," a play on the mathematical term "googol," which signifies the number 1 followed by 100 zeros. This name choice underscored the search engine's mission to organise the vast amount of information available on the internet. Google was officially incorporated as a company in September 1998, and its meteoric rise to prominence began. Since then, it has flourished into one of the world's leading providers of search engines and other essential technologies used by millions across the globe every day. With its ongoing innovation and commitment to excellence and customer service, Google Search will continue to be at the pinnacle of internet searches for years to come.

At its launch, Google Search had an index of only 25 million web pages, which was a fraction of what other search engines had at the time. However, its innovative

PageRank algorithm, which analysed the quality and relevance of web pages, quickly made it a hit among users. Google's search results were much more accurate and relevant than those of other search engines, which quickly led to its popularity and growth.

Google stays ahead of the competition by continuously innovating and improving its product offerings. Whether it's new features like voice search or something as simple as improved loading speeds, Google puts time and resources into ensuring that its platform remains up-to-date and relevant for users around the world.

In the early years, Google Search continued to improve and expand its features. In 2000, Google introduced AdWords, a system that allowed advertisers to bid on keywords to display their ads alongside search results. AdWords was a game-changer for online advertising, and it quickly became a major revenue source for Google. In 2001, Google introduced Google Images, which allowed users to search for images on the web. This feature quickly became popular among users and helped Google cement its position as the leading search engine.

Over the years, Google has continued to innovate and expand its features. In 2004, Google introduced Google Scholar, a search engine that focused on academic papers and research. In 2005, Google Maps was introduced, revolutionising online mapping and location-based services. In 2006, Google introduced Google Trends, which allowed users to see how often particular search terms were entered into Google's search engine.

One of the biggest milestones in the history of Google Search came in 2010 when Google introduced Google Instant. Google Instant was a feature that displayed search results as a user typed in their query, providing instant search suggestions and results. This feature was a game-changer for the search experience, making it much faster and more intuitive.

Today, Google Search processes over 3.5 billion searches per day, accounting for more than 90% of the global search engine market share. Its influence on the digital landscape is immense, shaping how businesses approach online marketing and how consumers access information. But what exactly is it that makes Google so successful? It's all thanks to the algorithm that powers their search engine. Over the years, Google has developed and refined its algorithm to provide users with the best possible results for their queries.

At its core, Google's Search algorithm is designed to understand queries that are entered into its system and provide relevant results. To do this, it uses a combination of natural language processing and machine learning techniques to detect patterns in user queries and match them with relevant web pages. For example, if someone searches for "how does a refrigerator work," Google's algorithm will analyse the query and identify words like "refrigerator" and "work." It then uses these words to identify web pages that contain information about refrigerators and their functioning.

The Google search algorithm is a complex set of rules used by Google to determine which websites should be displayed for any given query. It considers numerous factors, including relevance, freshness, keyword density, user location, and more. The algorithm also uses algorithms such as PageRank to prioritise pages based on their importance relative to other pages on a website. This helps ensure that only authoritative websites are listed in response to a query.

Through refining its algorithms and adding new features, Google has consistently improved its ability to deliver relevant results. One such feature is Universal Search, which launched in 2007 and allows users to view images, videos, news items, shopping results, books and flight information alongside traditional web pages when they search using specific keywords. This feature was later expanded upon with the introduction of Knowledge Graphs in 2012, which help answer questions without requiring extra clicks or navigating away from the main search page. Over the years, Google has introduced several major algorithm updates to improve search quality and combat manipulative SEO practices.

The first major algorithm update was the Google Panda algorithm, introduced in 2011, which marked a significant shift in the world of search engine optimisation (SEO) and profoundly impacted the digital marketing landscape. This update aimed to improve the quality of search results by penalising low-quality content and rewarding websites with original, valuable content.

The objective of the Panda algorithm was to address the growing issue of low-quality content proliferating on the internet. Prior to the Panda update, many websites, known as "content farms," would churn out large volumes of poorly written, thin, or duplicate content solely designed to rank for specific keywords. These content farms often achieved high search rankings despite offering little value to users, compromising the overall quality of search results.

The Panda update sought to rectify this situation by evaluating websites based on the quality and originality of their content. By favouring websites with well-researched, informative, and engaging content, Google aimed to provide users with a more valuable and satisfactory search experience.

The introduction of the Panda algorithm had several important implications for businesses and their digital marketing strategies. One of the key takeaways highlighted the need for a holistic approach to digital marketing, with SEO and content marketing strategies working in tandem to achieve optimal results. By focusing on creating high-quality content that appeals to users and incorporates relevant keywords, businesses can improve their search rankings, drive organic traffic, and establish themselves as industry authorities.

The Google Panda algorithm has had a lasting impact on the digital marketing landscape, emphasising the importance of quality content and user experience in achieving search engine success. By understanding the objectives and implications of the Panda update, businesses can adapt their marketing strategies to align with Google's emphasis on content quality and user experience, positioning themselves for long-term success in the increasingly competitive online environment.

The second notable update was the Google Penguin algorithm, launched in 2012, which further refined the search engine's ranking criteria by targeting manipulative link-building practices and rewarding websites with natural, high-quality backlink profiles. This update was built on the principles established by the Panda algorithm, emphasising the importance of ethical SEO strategies and promoting a more equitable digital ecosystem.

The main objective of the Penguin algorithm was to address the widespread issue of inorganic and manipulative link-building practices that were undermining the integrity of search rankings. Prior to the Penguin update, many websites sought to exploit the search engine's reliance on backlinks as a key ranking factor by employing tactics such as buying links, participating in link schemes, and utilising low-quality or spammy websites to generate backlinks. These practices allowed websites to artificially inflate their search rankings, often at the expense of more deserving sites with legitimate, high-quality backlink profiles.

The Penguin algorithm aimed to level the playing field by identifying and penalising websites that engaged in manipulative link-building practices. By analysing the quality and relevance of a website's backlinks and the overall link profile, the Penguin algorithm sought to reward websites with natural, organic backlinks and penalise those that relied on artificial means to manipulate their rankings.

The Google Penguin algorithm has played a pivotal role in shaping the digital marketing landscape by targeting manipulative link-building practices and promoting ethical SEO strategies. This update helped businesses adopt Google's emphasis on high-quality, natural backlinks and maintain a strong online presence in the face of ongoing algorithmic changes. As the digital ecosystem continues to evolve, businesses must remain vigilant and adapt to new best practices to stay ahead of the competition and achieve long-term success.

In 2013, Google introduced the Hummingbird algorithm; it marked another significant milestone in the evolution of search engine algorithms and the digital marketing landscape. This update aimed to improve the search engine's ability to understand user intent and provide more accurate, relevant search results by focusing on the meaning behind search queries rather than relying solely on keyword matching.

The aim of the Hummingbird algorithm was to enhance Google's understanding of user intent and provide more accurate, relevant search results by considering the context and meaning behind search queries. Prior to the Hummingbird update, search engines primarily relied on keyword matching to determine the relevance of web pages to specific queries. This approach, while effective to some extent, often failed to account for the nuanced meaning and context behind users' search terms, resulting in less-than-optimal search results.

The Hummingbird algorithm sought to rectify this situation by incorporating semantic search principles, which focus on the meaning and context of search queries rather than simple keyword matching. By analysing the relationships between words and phrases within queries and considering factors such as user location and search history, the Hummingbird algorithm aimed to provide a more defined understanding of user intent and deliver more accurate, relevant search results. This algorithm has played a critical role in shaping the digital marketing landscape by promoting a more user-centric, intent-driven approach to SEO and content marketing.

The naming convention of Google's algorithms after animals stems from the company's desire to create a memorable and relatable association for each major update. These names serve as a mnemonic device that makes it easier for the digital marketing and SEO community to reference, discuss, and remember the specific changes and implications of each algorithmic update. By assigning animal names to these updates, Google effectively creates a more approachable and accessible means for professionals and the general public to engage with the intricacies of the search engine's constantly evolving ranking criteria. Additionally, the names often reflect the overall theme or purpose of the update, subtly encapsulating its intended impact on the search ecosystem.

The first non-animal named algorithm was introduced in 2015, the Google Mobilegeddon algorithm. This signified a major shift in the search engine's ranking criteria, placing greater emphasis on the importance of mobile-friendliness in determining search rankings. This update acknowledged the growing prevalence of mobile internet usage and aimed to provide a better search experience for users accessing the web from smartphones and other mobile devices.

The primary objective of the Mobilegeddon algorithm was to enhance the search experience for mobile users by prioritising mobile-friendly websites in search engine results. With the rapid rise of mobile internet usage and the increasing reliance on smartphones and other mobile devices for accessing information, Google recognised the need to ensure that search results were tailored to the needs and preferences of this growing user base.

The Mobilegeddon algorithm assessed the mobile-friendliness of websites based on several criteria, including responsive design, fast loading times, and ease of navigation on mobile devices. By incorporating these factors into its ranking algorithm, Google aimed to promote the adoption of mobile-friendly design practices and ensure that mobile users were provided with search results that were both relevant and easily accessible on their devices.

The Google Mobilegeddon algorithm has played a critical role in shaping the digital marketing landscape by emphasising the importance of mobile-friendliness and mobile optimisation in the search engine ranking process.

Alongside the Google Mobilegeddon update in 2015, Google also introduced RankBrain. The Google RankBrain algorithm represented a major leap forward in the search engine's ability to understand and process complex, nuanced search queries by incorporating machine learning and artificial intelligence (AI). This update aimed to enhance the search experience by delivering more accurate, relevant search results for users, particularly for those with unique or previously unencountered search queries. In this section, we will examine the RankBrain algorithm, its objectives, its impact on the SEO industry, and its implications for businesses in the digital marketing sphere.

The primary objective of the RankBrain algorithm was to improve Google's understanding of user intent and provide more accurate, relevant search results by leveraging machine learning and AI. RankBrain was designed to analyse and process complex, multi-faceted search queries that may not have been encountered before, thereby enabling the search engine to adapt to new search trends and user behaviours more effectively.

By incorporating AI and machine learning into its ranking algorithm, Google aimed to enhance its ability to interpret the context and meaning behind search queries and identify relationships between seemingly unrelated concepts. This allowed the search engine to provide more accurate, relevant search results, even for highly specific or unusual search terms.

The Google RankBrain algorithm has played a critical role in shaping the digital marketing landscape by emphasising the importance of user intent, context, and semantic search in the search engine ranking process. By understanding the objectives and implications of the RankBrain update, businesses can adapt their marketing strategies to align with Google's focus on delivering accurate, relevant search results and ensure that their content remains engaging, valuable, and visible in the digital ecosystem. As search engines continue to evolve and incorporate more advanced AI and machine learning technologies, businesses must stay informed and be prepared to adapt their marketing practices to maintain a strong online presence and achieve long-term success.

The Google BERT (Bidirectional Encoder Representations from Transformers) algorithm, introduced in 2019, marked a significant advancement in the search engine's ability to understand and process natural language, particularly in relation to the context and nuance of search queries. BERT, which stands for Bidirectional Encoder Representations from Transformers, is a natural language processing (NLP) model that employs deep learning techniques to improve the search engine's comprehension of human language.

The objective of the BERT algorithm was to enhance Google's understanding of the intricacies of natural language and provide more accurate, relevant search results by leveraging advanced NLP techniques. BERT was specifically designed to improve the search engine's ability to interpret the context and meaning of complex search queries, including those that involve prepositions, pronouns, and other linguistic elements that can significantly impact the interpretation of a sentence.

By incorporating the BERT model into its ranking algorithm, Google aimed to enhance its ability to interpret and process natural language more effectively, allowing the search engine to provide more accurate, relevant search results for a wide range of search queries, particularly those that may have been difficult to understand or parse using previous algorithms.

The Google BERT algorithm has played a critical role in shaping the digital marketing landscape by emphasising the importance of natural language understanding, context, and semantic search in the search engine ranking process. By understanding the objectives and implications of the BERT update, businesses can adapt their marketing strategies to align with Google's focus on delivering accurate, relevant search results and ensure that their content remains engaging, valuable, and visible in the digital ecosystem. As search engines continue to evolve and incorporate more advanced NLP and machine learning technologies, businesses must stay informed and be prepared to adapt their marketing practices to maintain a strong online presence and achieve long-term success.

Google Search continues to evolve and improve with the passing of time. In 2018, Google introduced a new feature called People Also Ask, which displays related questions asked by other people to help users find more information about their query. This is augmented by its BERT technology which uses natural language processing to better understand user queries and provide more accurate results. Additionally, Google has introduced deeper integrations with its other products, such as Maps and YouTube, which display relevant search results and allow users to directly access these services from within the main search page.

The current landscape of the Google Search algorithm significantly differs from past versions. It relies heavily on leveraging artificial intelligence and machine learning to understand searcher intent, break down searches into topics and concepts, and make proactive suggestions for related queries. This allows Google to better understand a user's context when making a request, allowing for more accurate rankings of search results. Google has also taken steps to reduce its reliance on keyword-based indexing. Instead, it evaluates user engagement signals such as clicks and dwell time to help evaluate the relevance of search engine result pages (SERP). This expanded understanding of user intent provides users with highly relevant results and translates into better overall online experiences.

With the rise of the digital age, it has become increasingly important to ensure that one's website is ranked highly on search engines such as Google. Therefore, it is essential to understand what factors influence a website's ranking in Google. Factors range from having a website that loads quickly and is mobile-friendly to having high-quality content which provides value and relevance to topics related to one's business; this includes optimising titles, descriptions, URLs and internal links with keywords. It is also important for websites to have social media sharing capabilities and an effective link structure so visitors can easily navigate the website. By being aware of these ranking factors on

Google search engine websites, businesses are able to maximise visibility when potential customers search for them online.

However, Google has also implemented a ranking algorithm that takes advertising into consideration when displaying search results, making it even more important for businesses to add marketing to their campaigns. This new approach adds great importance to advertisement optimisation and keyword relevance. Companies must now pay special attention to the content of their advertising campaigns, as this will be considered every time a user searches for related terms. Companies can take advantage of this opportunity to increase their visibility and gain even more customers through strong and well-targeted advertisements by paying close attention to what users are looking for.

Advertising on the Google search algorithm is growing in importance as more and more marketing strategists turn to digital technology to reach their target audiences. This type of advertising allows for higher levels of user engagement and offers insight into how their ads perform. By targeting certain keywords, companies also have much more control over the kind of output they receive from the searches. This can lead to a far better return on investment than those generated from traditional marketing methods. Furthermore, by enabling marketers to reach prospective customers further down the buying funnel, online advertising has become essential to any comprehensive marketing strategy.

With the current digital landscape and social media platforms, companies are increasingly looking to advertise within search engine results to grow their customer base. However, this presents challenges of its own due to the need for the content to be tailored to the specific search query to captivate consumer attention. Also, as noted by experts in the field, search engine algorithms prioritise certain forms of content over other forms when placing ads amidst their results. As such, it can be difficult for businesses without a strong online presence or knowledge of keyword optimisation techniques to push their advertising reach successfully. Despite these struggles though, various strategies still exist for companies wishing to place an effective advertising campaign within a search environment.

In today's world, it is difficult to imagine how anyone ever survived without easily accessible information provided by a simple Google search. With the touch of a button, we can quickly browse through articles, images, and videos related to topics of any kind. Google has drastically changed how we access knowledge and data, allowing us to learn more in less time than ever before. This technology undoubtedly revolutionised our day-to-day lives by granting us quick and convenient access to previously inaccessible information.

What was once a laborious task of looking through books and archives has become much simpler. With the help of Google's sophisticated algorithms, users can quickly search for the answers to virtually any query with just a few clicks. Moreover, it offers valuable insights into popular trends and helps businesses identify new opportunities on emerging topics. As our reliance on efficient data search continues to grow, Google remains at the cutting edge of providing an unparalleled user experience for its users.

In the years since Google was founded in 1998, its search capabilities have grown exponentially. Search has now become an integral part of everyday life for people worldwide, providing easy access to information that may have been difficult or nearly impossible to obtain before. Google's ever-improving algorithms result in increasingly accurate results being returned for searches - something that seemed unimaginable when Google began its mission to organise the world's information 20 short years ago.

With powerful tools such as these at our fingertips, it is no surprise that so many of us rely on Google search to help us with our day-to-day lives.

With numerous advancements in the world of technology, Google Search is looking to the future of its services. Google has a history of innovation and improvement that it looks to continue as the years go on. The uses and features that have been presented by Google Search have revolutionised how we access information today, so one can only imagine what new capabilities may be utilised in the near future. With dedicated researchers and engineers hard at work, customers should expect more efficient, faster, and structured approaches to searching for answers regarding any topic. This ultimately leads to providing users with more accurate information in a shorter time frame than ever before. As we step into a new era of technology developments, we will likely see Google continuing its rapid expansion within the industry as they seek out further opportunities that improve search capabilities worldwide.

Chapter Two: Utilising Google Search for Your Business

In today's increasingly interconnected world, Google Search has emerged as a critical tool for businesses to remain competitive and thrive. Employing the vast array of resources offered by Google Search allows businesses to gain a better understanding of their target audience, optimise their online presence, and increase visibility to potential customers. Effectively leveraging the power of Google Search will increase brand awareness, drive meaningful customer engagement, and foster growth. From improving organic search rankings to harnessing the potential of paid advertising, Google Search offers a myriad of opportunities for businesses to succeed in the digital landscape.

The platform's ubiquity and dominance in the search engine market are paramount to utilising Google Search for your business. With billions of users worldwide, Google Search provides unparalleled access to a vast array of potential customers. Ensuring that your business is easily discoverable on this platform is a crucial step towards success in the digital realm.

In the contemporary digital landscape, Google Search serves as a powerful tool for businesses to reach out to a global audience, enhance their visibility, and drive growth. Given its vast scope and application, it is now more critical than ever for businesses to understand how to fully harness the potential of Google Search. By doing so, they can stay ahead in an increasingly competitive environment and make the most of this expansive database.

The impact of Google Search on business visibility and growth cannot be overstated. As the world's leading search engine, Google processes billions of search queries daily, guiding users to relevant websites, products, and services. For businesses, achieving high visibility on Google Search can significantly improve their online presence, attract new customers, and expand their market share. Consequently, understanding and implementing search engine optimisation (SEO) strategies is essential for businesses aiming to increase their online visibility and foster growth.

Search engines play a pivotal role in the modern digital marketplace, as they help users navigate the vast amount of information available on the internet. By organising and ranking websites based on their relevance to a given search query, search engines like Google enable users to find the information, products, or services they seek. For businesses, being visible on search engines is vital for success in the digital age, allowing them to reach a broader audience, generate leads, and grow their customer base. By optimising their website for search engines, businesses can enhance their online presence, boost organic traffic, and establish their credibility in the eyes of potential customers.

Google Search empowers businesses to identify and comprehend the needs and desires of their customers. By conducting thorough keyword research, businesses can discover the specific terms and phrases customers are searching for. This information can then be used to craft targeted content, products, and services that cater to these needs, ultimately enhancing customer satisfaction and loyalty.

Understanding customer intent is essential for creating content that resonates with your audience. By analysing search queries and user behaviour, you can identify patterns and trends that indicate customer pain points and preferences. This insight allows you to tailor your offerings to better address the needs of your target market, ultimately leading to higher conversion rates and increased customer satisfaction.

To fully harness the potential of Google Search, businesses must first identify their target audience's needs and preferences. This process involves researching the demographic, psychographic, and behavioural characteristics of potential customers. By deeply understanding their target audience, businesses can tailor their SEO and marketing strategies to appeal to their unique needs.

Keyword research is a fundamental aspect of understanding a business's target audience. It involves identifying the search terms that potential customers will likely use when looking for products or services related to a business. By analysing the popularity, competition, and relevance of these keywords, businesses can develop an effective SEO strategy that targets the most appropriate search terms. This in-depth understanding of customer needs allows businesses to create content and marketing materials that truly resonate with their audience, resulting in higher engagement and conversion rates.

A comprehensive understanding of the target audience goes beyond keyword research. It is crucial to analyse search intent and user behaviour, as this provides insight into what potential customers are looking for and how they interact with search engines. By evaluating metrics such as bounce rate, time on site, and click-through rate, businesses can identify areas of improvement and optimise their website content to engage users better and meet their needs.

Understanding search intent and user behaviour is crucial for creating content and SEO strategies that resonate with the target audience. Search intent refers to the reason behind a user's search query, such as informational, navigational, commercial, or transactional intent. By analysing user behaviour and search intent, businesses can create content that addresses the needs and desires of their target audience, increasing the likelihood of ranking higher in search results and attracting more organic traffic.

Implementing effective SEO strategies is crucial to improving your ranking on SERPs. This includes techniques such as building high-quality backlinks, optimising meta tags and title tags, and incorporating structured data to make your website more accessible to search engines. By consistently implementing SEO best practices, businesses can increase their visibility on Google Search, attract more organic traffic, and drive customer acquisition and retention.

Competitor analysis and benchmarking are other critical aspects of understanding a business's target audience. By analysing competitors' online presence, businesses can gain insights into what works and what doesn't, identify gaps in the market, and adapt their strategies accordingly.

Tools such as SEMrush and Ahrefs can help businesses to conduct competitor analysis and benchmarking. These tools can provide businesses with insights into their competitors' SEO strategies, the keywords they are targeting, and their online performance.

On-page optimisation techniques involve optimising the content and structure of your website to make it more visible and relevant to search engines. This includes optimising page titles, meta descriptions, header tags, and image alt tags, as well as ensuring that your website content is high-quality, original, and relevant to your target audience.

Off-page optimisation techniques involve optimising external factors that impact your website's visibility and ranking in search engine results in pages. This includes building high-quality backlinks from reputable websites, as well as leveraging social media and other online platforms to drive traffic and engagement to your website.

Technical SEO involves optimising the technical aspects of your website to ensure that it is structured and coded in a way that is easily accessible and visible to search engines. This includes optimising website speed and performance, ensuring that your website is mobile-friendly, and implementing structured data markup to improve search engine visibility and usability.

Search engine optimisation (SEO) is the practice of optimising your website and online content to improve your visibility and ranking in search engine results pages. A strong SEO strategy is essential for businesses looking to improve their online presence and attract more targeted traffic to their website.

Google Search empowers businesses to identify and comprehend the needs and desires of their customers. By conducting thorough keyword research, businesses can discover the specific terms and phrases customers are searching for. This information can then be used to craft targeted content, products, and services that cater to these needs, ultimately enhancing customer satisfaction and loyalty.

Understanding customer intent is essential for creating content that resonates with your audience. By analysing search queries and user behaviour, you can identify patterns and trends that indicate customer pain points and preferences. This insight allows you to tailor your offerings to better address the needs of your target market, ultimately leading to higher conversion rates and increased customer satisfaction.

To rank higher on Google Search, businesses must ensure their website content is both relevant and engaging. This involves creating high-quality, informative content that addresses the needs of your target audience while incorporating relevant keywords in a natural and organic manner. Optimising your content not only improves your search engine ranking but also increases the likelihood that visitors to your site will become customers.

Businesses should also consider factors such as website structure, user experience, and page load speed. These elements play a significant role in how Google ranks websites and can greatly impact your search engine visibility. Optimising website content not only involves incorporating relevant keywords but also ensuring that the content is well-organised, easily navigable, and visually appealing. This enhances the user experience, which is an essential factor in Google's ranking algorithm.

Regularly monitoring and analysing a website's performance is crucial for businesses looking to maximise their online presence. Google offers various analytical tools that enable businesses to identify successful ad campaigns, trends in keyword searches, and other data insights that can be beneficial for their marketing efforts. By leveraging these tools, businesses can make data-driven decisions to refine their strategies and enhance their online visibility.

Google Analytics, for example, provides businesses with comprehensive information on their website traffic, user behaviour, and conversion rates. This information can be used to identify areas of improvement, track the success of marketing campaigns, and gauge the effectiveness of SEO efforts.

Utilising Google's suite of analytical tools, such as Google Analytics and Google Search Console, businesses can monitor the performance of their online presence, ad campaigns, and website. These tools provide invaluable insights into user behaviour, keyword trends, and the overall success of your marketing efforts. By regularly reviewing this data, you can identify areas for improvement and adjust your strategies accordingly to ensure continued growth and success.

Setting up local listings for your business on Google Maps and Google My Business can greatly enhance your visibility to customers searching for products or services in your area. By providing accurate and up-to-date information such as your business address, phone number, operating hours, and customer reviews, you can improve your search ranking in local results and make it easier for potential customers to find and engage with your business.

In addition to basic information, businesses can also utilise Google My Business features like posting updates, showcasing products or services, and managing customer reviews. Responding to reviews, both positive and negative, demonstrates your commitment to customer satisfaction and helps build trust with your audience.

In conclusion, the effective utilisation of Google Search is paramount for businesses to thrive in today's digital landscape. By understanding the importance of search engines in the modern marketplace, identifying and comprehending the needs of your target audience, developing a comprehensive SEO strategy, leveraging Google Ads for growth, and focusing on local SEO and Google My Business, businesses can significantly boost their online visibility and reach a broader customer base.

Moreover, the continuous monitoring of performance metrics and KPIs using tools like Google Analytics and Google Search Console enables businesses to identify areas for improvement, adapt their strategies, and optimise their online presence. By embracing these best practices and integrating them into a cohesive digital marketing approach, businesses can harness the full potential of

Google Search, driving sustainable growth and success in an increasingly interconnected world.

Chapter Three: Understanding AI

In the ever-evolving landscape of technology, the concept of artificial intelligence (AI) has emerged as a prominent area of research and development, imbued with the potential to revolutionise various aspects of human life. The ultimate objective of AI research encompasses developing intelligent systems adept at executing tasks ordinarily requiring human ingenuity. The following sections elucidate the intricacies of AI, its definition, evolution, types, applications, and the mechanisms that underpin its functionality while also drawing comparisons between AI and human intelligence.

Artificial intelligence, a multidisciplinary field within computer science, encompasses the design and creation of machines capable of emulating human-like cognitive abilities such as learning, problem-solving, decision-making, and natural language comprehension. The overarching objective of AI research is to develop intelligent systems that can perform tasks traditionally associated with human intellect.

Artificial intelligence can be characterised as the capacity of a machine or computer program to think, reason, and learn in a manner akin to human intelligence. This entails processing vast amounts of data, discerning patterns, making decisions based on those patterns, and adjusting behaviour according to new information or experiences. The term "artificial intelligence" itself indicates the intention to construct a non-biological entity that possesses cognitive capabilities.

The concept of AI emerged as early as ancient history, with myths and legends featuring artificial beings endowed with intelligence. However, the formal pursuit of artificial intelligence began in the mid-20th century, prompted by the development of electronic computers. Early AI research sought to imbue machines with reasoning and problem-solving abilities, focusing on symbolic manipulation and rule-based systems.

It became apparent that capturing the complexity and versatility of human intelligence in a machine was an immensely challenging endeavour. Nevertheless, advances in computer hardware, algorithms, and machine learning techniques have enabled significant strides in the development of AI systems, facilitating remarkable accomplishments in areas such as natural language processing, computer vision, and robotics.

The field of artificial intelligence has witnessed remarkable progress since its inception in the mid-20th century. The early years of AI research were marked by the development of symbolic AI, which focused on creating rule-based systems that relied on logical reasoning to perform tasks. These systems were primarily designed to solve problems in domains such as mathematics, logic, and chess.

The field of artificial intelligence has undergone a fascinating evolution since its inception. Early AI research in the 1950s and 1960s revolved around symbolic AI, also known as "good old-fashioned artificial intelligence" (GOFAI), which relied on explicit rules and logic to solve problems. Despite initial optimism, the limitations of this approach became evident as it struggled to handle complex, real-world situations.

In the 1980s, AI research shifted its focus to knowledge-based systems, also known as expert systems, which aimed to replicate the decision-making processes of human experts by incorporating vast amounts of domain-specific knowledge. These systems demonstrated considerable success in specialised fields such as medicine, geology, and finance.

The 1990s marked a significant shift in AI research with the introduction of machine learning techniques, such as neural networks and genetic algorithms. These methods enabled computers to learn from data and adapt their behaviour, leading to substantial advancements in AI capabilities.

The advent of the internet and the exponential growth of data in the 21st century ushered in a new era of AI research, characterised by the development of data-driven techniques such as machine learning and deep learning. These approaches have enabled AI systems to learn from vast datasets and perform complex tasks with unprecedented accuracy, resulting in groundbreaking achievements in areas such as natural language processing, computer vision, and autonomous vehicles.

In recent years, breakthroughs in deep learning and reinforcement learning have propelled AI to new heights, empowering systems to perform exceptionally well in tasks like image and speech recognition, natural language processing, and game-playing. The rise of big data, cloud computing, and specialised hardware, such as GPUs, has further accelerated AI development by providing the necessary computational resources and data to train increasingly sophisticated models.

Artificial intelligence is a multifaceted field that encompasses a wide range of techniques, approaches, and applications. To better understand the various forms of AI, it is helpful to classify them into distinct categories based on their capabilities and underlying technologies. This section will delve into the different types of AI, discussing their characteristics and providing examples of their practical applications.

Narrow AI, also called weak AI, is designed to perform specific tasks or solve narrowly defined problems. These AI systems do not possess general intelligence or the ability to understand or learn tasks outside their specific domain. Examples of narrow AI include speech recognition systems, chatbots, and recommendation engines. Despite their limitations, narrow AI systems have demonstrated remarkable success in their respective areas, revolutionising industries such as customer service, e-commerce, and transportation.

In contrast, general AI, or strong AI, aims to develop machines that can perform any intellectual task a human being can do. While this type of AI remains largely theoretical, researchers are continuously working towards creating systems that can learn, reason, and adapt across multiple domains, similar to human intelligence. The development of general AI would have profound implications for society, potentially leading to breakthroughs in fields such as healthcare, education, and scientific research.

Another classification of AI involves the distinction between symbolic AI and subsymbolic AI. Symbolic AI, also known as classical AI or rule-based AI, relies on explicit representations of knowledge and logic to perform tasks. This approach typically involves the creation of formal systems that manipulate symbols to solve problems, such as expert systems and rule-based reasoning engines.

Subsymbolic AI, on the other hand, is focused on modelling the underlying mechanisms and processes of human cognition. Techniques within this category include connectionist approaches, such as neural networks and deep learning, which seek to emulate the structure and function of the human brain. Subsymbolic AI has gained significant traction in recent years, leading to breakthroughs in areas such as image recognition, natural language processing, and game-playing.

Machine learning, a subfield of AI, is the process of training computers to learn from data and improve their performance on specific tasks without being explicitly programmed. This approach enables AI systems to adapt and refine their behaviour based on new information or experiences, leading to more accurate and effective outcomes over time.

One of the key techniques within machine learning is the use of neural networks, computational models inspired by the structure and function of biological neural networks in the human brain. Neural networks consist of interconnected nodes, or neurons, that process input data and transmit signals to other nodes through weighted connections. By adjusting these weights during a training process, the neural network can learn to recognise patterns and make predictions based on input data.

Deep learning, a subset of machine learning, involves the use of deep neural networks with multiple layers of neurons. These complex architectures enable the extraction of higher-level features and representations from raw data, allowing for more sophisticated and nuanced predictions. Deep learning has been responsible for many recent advancements in AI, particularly in fields such as image and speech recognition, natural language understanding, and game-playing.

Developing AI algorithms is a complex and iterative process that involves multiple stages, requiring the collaborative efforts of computer scientists, data analysts, and domain experts.

To begin with, data collection plays a crucial role in the development of AI algorithms. Machine learning models, which form the backbone of most AI systems, rely on vast amounts of data to learn and make predictions. Consequently, data scientists must gather large datasets that accurately represent the problem domain, ensuring that the data is diverse, balanced, and representative of real-world scenarios.

Once the data has been collected, it undergoes a preprocessing stage. In this phase, data scientists clean, preprocess, and transform the data to ensure that it is suitable for the selected algorithm. This may involve removing duplicates, handling missing values, normalising data, or encoding categorical variables. Preprocessing is critical in ensuring that the data is in a format that can be easily understood and processed by the machine learning model.

The next step in AI algorithm development is selecting an appropriate algorithm or model. Researchers and developers must carefully consider various factors, such as the type of problem being addressed, the nature of the data, and the desired outcome, to determine the most suitable algorithm. This may involve choosing between supervised or unsupervised learning, selecting a specific type of neural network, or opting for a more specialised approach, such as reinforcement learning.

With the data preprocessed and the algorithm selected, the training phase commences. In this stage, the machine learning model is fed the training data and learns patterns and relationships within the data. As the model processes the data, it adjusts its internal parameters to minimise errors and improve its predictive capabilities. The training process may involve numerous iterations as the model continues to refine its understanding of the data.

After the model has been trained, it must be evaluated to assess its performance and accuracy. This involves testing the model on a separate dataset, known as the validation or testing set, which was not used during training. The evaluation process helps developers identify potential issues, such as overfitting or underfitting and provides insight into the model's generalisability to new, unseen data.

Finally, based on the evaluation results, developers may refine and optimise the AI algorithm, making adjustments to improve its performance, address any identified issues, and ensure that the model is well-suited to the problem at hand. This iterative process continues until the AI algorithm meets the desired level of accuracy and performance.

Artificial intelligence and human intelligence, though sharing similarities in their abilities to process information and make decisions, exhibit several fundamental differences that set them apart.

One of the most fundamental differences between AI and human intelligence lies in the way they process information. Human intelligence is inherently linked to our biological makeup, encompassing our neural networks, brain chemistry, and cognitive abilities. Our intelligence is shaped by both genetic factors and environmental influences, allowing us to learn and adapt to new situations through a complex interplay of nature and nurture. In contrast, artificial intelligence is built on computational systems and algorithms, with machine learning models and neural networks designed to simulate the way humans process information. However, AI systems are limited by the data and algorithms they are provided with and cannot naturally acquire knowledge or adapt to new situations in the same way that humans can.

Another key difference between AI and human intelligence is the scope of their capabilities. While AI systems excel in specific, narrowly defined tasks, such as image recognition or language translation, they often struggle with more complex, multi-faceted problems that require a deep understanding of context, nuance, and human emotions. Human intelligence, on the other hand, is capable of handling a wide range of tasks, from abstract problem-solving to social interactions, thanks to our innate capacity for empathy, creativity, and critical thinking. This versatility allows humans to navigate the complexities of the world and adapt to new challenges in ways that AI systems currently cannot.

Moreover, the speed and efficiency at which AI systems can process information and perform tasks often surpass human capabilities. Due to the computational nature of artificial intelligence, machines can process vast amounts of data, recognise patterns, and make decisions at a much faster rate than humans, who are limited by the speed of their biological neural networks. This advantage allows AI systems to excel in areas such as data analysis, optimisation, and automation, where speed and accuracy are of the utmost importance.

Ethics and morality also play a significant role in differentiating AI from human intelligence. Human intelligence is intrinsically tied to our moral and ethical values, which guide our decision-making and behaviour. These values are shaped by a combination of cultural, societal, and personal factors, leading to a diverse range of beliefs and perspectives across different individuals and communities. In contrast, AI systems do not possess inherent ethical or moral values, and any attempt to instil these values in machines depends on the input and guidance of their human creators. This raises complex questions about the role of ethics in AI development, the potential biases in AI systems, and the responsibility of AI creators to ensure that their systems align with societal values and norms.

The history of artificial intelligence is a fascinating journey marked by groundbreaking innovations and a continuous drive to push the boundaries of human knowledge. It can be traced back to the early 20th century, with the pioneering work of mathematician and logician Alan Turing. In 1950, Turing proposed the Turing Test as a means to determine whether a machine could exhibit intelligent behaviour indistinguishable from that of a human. This seminal work laid the foundation for the development of artificial intelligence as a field of study.

The 1950s and 1960s saw the emergence of the first AI programs, such as Arthur Samuel's checkers-playing program and Joseph Weisenbaum's ELIZA, a natural language processing system that simulated a psychotherapist. These early AI systems demonstrated the potential for machines to learn and interact with humans, sparking widespread interest and investment in AI research.

In the 1970s, AI research shifted towards the development of knowledge-based systems, which relied on formal logic and symbolic representations to solve problems. One of the most notable examples of this approach was the development of MYCIN, an expert system designed to diagnose infectious diseases. Although these systems showed promise, they were limited by their reliance on hand-coded knowledge and their inability to learn from experience.

The 1980s and 1990s brought renewed interest in AI, driven by advances in computer hardware and the emergence of new machine learning techniques. During this period, AI researchers began to explore the potential of neural networks, which are computational models inspired by the structure and function of the human brain. Neural networks allow machines to learn from data and adapt their behaviour, paving the way for a new generation of AI systems.

The 21st century has seen an explosion in AI research and applications, fueled by the increasing availability of large datasets and the development of powerful new algorithms. Breakthroughs such as IBM's Deep Blue, which defeated world chess champion Garry Kasparov in 1997, and Google DeepMind's AlphaGo, which defeated the world Go champion Lee Sedol in 2016, have showcased the growing capabilities of AI systems. Meanwhile, advances in natural language processing, computer vision, and robotics have led to the creation of increasingly sophisticated AI applications, from virtual assistants like Siri and Alexa to self-driving cars and drones.

The field of artificial intelligence has experienced rapid growth and development in recent years, with significant breakthroughs and advancements transforming the way we perceive and interact with technology.

One of the most notable achievements in AI research has been the development of advanced natural language processing (NLP) models, such as OpenAI's GPT-3. These models have revolutionised the way machines understand and interact with human language, enabling AI systems to generate human-like text, translate languages with remarkable accuracy, and answer complex questions based on contextual understanding. The potential applications of NLP models are vast, spanning industries such as healthcare, education, customer service, and content creation.

In the realm of computer vision, AI research has yielded significant breakthroughs in image recognition and object detection. Deep learning techniques, such as convolutional neural networks (CNNs), have enabled machines to identify objects within images and videos with remarkable accuracy, approaching or even surpassing human-level performance in some cases. These advancements have widespread implications for industries such as security and surveillance, autonomous vehicles, and medical imaging, where accurate object identification is crucial.

Reinforcement learning, a subset of machine learning focused on training AI agents to make decisions based on trial and error, has also seen significant progress in recent years. Notable projects such as DeepMind's AlphaGo and AlphaZero have demonstrated the power of reinforcement learning in enabling AI systems to master complex games, such as Go and chess, by learning from experience rather than relying on pre-programmed strategies. The success of reinforcement learning in these domains suggests promising applications in other areas, such as robotics, supply chain optimisation, and financial trading.

Another area of AI research that has gained considerable attention is the development of generative adversarial networks (GANs). GANs consist of two neural networks, a generator and a discriminator, that compete against each other to create realistic, synthetic data. This innovative approach has led to significant advancements in the generation of high-quality images, videos, and even 3D models, with potential applications in entertainment, advertising, and data augmentation for training other AI models.

The advancements in AI research have opened up a plethora of applications across various industries and sectors. In the healthcare industry, AI has demonstrated immense potential for improving patient outcomes and streamlining processes. From diagnostic imaging, where AI algorithms can identify diseases and anomalies with remarkable accuracy, to drug discovery, where AI can rapidly screen and analyse potential compounds, the applications of AI in healthcare are vast and hold promise for significant advancements in medical treatment and patient care.

In the automotive industry, the development of autonomous vehicles has been propelled by AI research in areas such as computer vision, sensor fusion, and reinforcement learning. These technologies enable vehicles to perceive their surroundings, make intelligent decisions, and navigate complex environments with minimal human intervention. The widespread adoption of autonomous vehicles has the potential to improve road safety, reduce traffic congestion, and revolutionise transportation as we know it.

One of the most significant contributions of AI to the marketing industry is the ability to analyse vast amounts of data at an unprecedented speed and accuracy. This data-driven approach has enabled marketers to gain valuable insights into consumer behaviour, preferences, and trends, empowering them to develop more targeted and personalised marketing strategies. For instance, AI-powered tools can segment audiences based on their online behaviour, demographic information, and interests, allowing marketers to deliver tailored content and advertisements that resonate with individual consumers.

Moreover, AI has revolutionised the field of search engine optimisation (SEO), which plays a crucial role in ensuring that businesses are visible and accessible to potential customers through Google Search. AI algorithms, such as Google's RankBrain and BERT, have significantly enhanced the search engine's ability to understand user intent and deliver more accurate, relevant search results. This development has necessitated a shift in SEO strategies, with marketers now focusing on creating high-quality, user-centric content that aligns with the ever-evolving ranking criteria of AI-driven search engines.

Another area where AI has made a substantial impact is in the realm of content creation and curation. AI-powered tools, such as natural language generation (NLG) algorithms, can now generate written content that is virtually indistinguishable from that produced by human authors. This technology enables marketers to produce a high volume of engaging, relevant content more efficiently, freeing up resources for other strategic marketing initiatives. Additionally, AI algorithms can curate personalised content recommendations for users based on their browsing history and preferences, leading to a more tailored and engaging user experience.

Artificial intelligence offers a wealth of benefits and opportunities, but it also presents challenges and potential drawbacks that must be considered. One significant advantage of AI is its ability to enhance efficiency and productivity. AI systems can process and analyse large amounts of data much faster than humans, resulting in faster decision-making and problem-solving. This increased speed and accuracy can lead to substantial cost savings, as well as improvements in product quality and customer satisfaction.

Another benefit of AI is its potential for personalisation and customisation. By analysing user data, AI algorithms can provide tailored recommendations, content, and experiences for individual users, resulting in more relevant and engaging interactions. This personalisation can lead to increased customer loyalty, higher conversion rates, and improved overall user experience.

AI also has the potential to drive innovation and open up new opportunities across various industries. By automating repetitive and mundane tasks, AI can free up human resources to focus on more strategic and creative endeavours. This shift in focus can lead to the development of new products, services, and business models, ultimately promoting economic growth and progress.

However, there are also drawbacks and concerns associated with the widespread adoption of AI. One major concern is the potential loss of jobs due to automation. As AI systems become more advanced and capable of performing tasks traditionally done by humans, there is a risk that many jobs will become obsolete, leading to unemployment and economic disruption.

Another concern is the ethical implications of AI development and usage. As AI systems become more integrated into our lives, questions arise regarding privacy, data security, and algorithmic bias. Ensuring that AI systems are designed and implemented in a way that aligns with societal values and norms is of utmost importance in order to prevent potential harm and discrimination.

As artificial intelligence continues to advance and permeate various aspects of our lives, a growing number of ethical considerations have emerged. Privacy is a paramount ethical concern in the realm of AI. As AI systems rely on vast amounts of data to function effectively, the collection, storage, and analysis of personal information have become increasingly prevalent. This raises questions about the extent to which AI technologies should be allowed to access and utilise personal data, as well as the measures that must be in place to protect individuals' privacy rights. Balancing the benefits of AI-driven personalisation and data-driven decision-making with the need to safeguard privacy is a complex challenge that demands thoughtful consideration and the development of robust regulatory frameworks.

Fairness and bias are also critical ethical concerns in the context of AI. AI algorithms are developed by humans, and as such, they may inadvertently introduce biases into their systems based on the data they are trained on or the pre-existing beliefs and perspectives of their creators. This can lead to AI systems that perpetuate and exacerbate existing inequalities and discriminatory practices, with potentially harmful consequences for marginalised and vulnerable populations. Addressing issues of fairness and bias in AI requires a commitment to transparency, diversity, and ongoing evaluation to ensure that AI systems are developed and deployed in a manner that promotes fairness and equality.

Accountability is another significant ethical consideration in the AI landscape. As AI systems become increasingly autonomous and capable of making decisions with far-reaching consequences, questions arise about who should be held responsible for these decisions and their outcomes. Is it the AI system itself, the developers who created it, or the organisations that deploy and utilise the technology? Establishing clear lines of accountability is essential for ensuring that AI systems are developed and used responsibly and that appropriate mechanisms are in place to address any unintended consequences or harms that may arise.

The potential consequences of unchecked AI proliferation also warrant ethical consideration. As AI technologies become more powerful and ubiquitous, there is a risk that they could be used for nefarious purposes or lead to unintended negative consequences. For example, AI-driven deep fake technology can be used to create realistic yet fabricated images and videos that can manipulate public opinion or be used for blackmail. Similarly, deploying autonomous weapons raises concerns about the ethical implications of machines making life-and-death decisions without human intervention. Preventing the misuse of AI and mitigating potential negative consequences requires a proactive and collaborative approach involving governments, private sector entities, and civil society organisations working together to develop and enforce ethical guidelines and regulations.

The future of artificial intelligence is laden with opportunities and challenges as technology continues to evolve and become increasingly integrated into various aspects of our lives. In terms of development, we can expect AI systems to become more sophisticated, capable of processing and understanding increasingly complex data, and adapting to new situations autonomously. This will likely lead to the creation of more advanced AI applications in various fields, including healthcare, transportation, finance, and education, among others.

As AI adoption becomes more widespread, we can anticipate a greater emphasis on the development of user-friendly interfaces and seamless integration with existing technologies. This will enable a broader range of individuals and organisations to leverage AI systems effectively, driving further innovation and progress across various industries.

As AI continues to advance, a host of potential risks and opportunities emerge. One of the most significant challenges lies in ensuring that AI technologies are developed and deployed ethically and responsibly, with due consideration given to the implications of AI on privacy, fairness, accountability, and the potential consequences of unchecked AI proliferation. Addressing these challenges will require a concerted effort from various stakeholders, including governments, private sector entities, and civil society organisations, to develop robust ethical frameworks and regulatory mechanisms that guide AI development and usage in a manner that aligns with societal values and safeguards human rights.

On the other hand, the future of AI also presents a wealth of opportunities for innovation and progress. The development of more advanced AI systems has the potential to revolutionise various industries, enabling new products, services, and business models that were previously unimaginable. This, in turn, can drive economic growth, improve living standards, and enhance overall human well-being. By harnessing the power of AI responsibly and ethically, we can unlock a world of possibilities for a more prosperous and equitable future.

As we progress into the future of AI, the role of humans remains crucial in ensuring that the technology is developed and used safely and responsibly. Collaboration between governments, businesses, academia, and civil society organisations is necessary to develop robust guidelines and regulations that govern AI development and deployment. In addition, as AI becomes more pervasive, the need for a workforce skilled in AI and related technologies become increasingly important. Ensuring that individuals are equipped with the necessary knowledge and skills to navigate the AI landscape will be essential for driving innovation and mitigating potential risks.

AI systems should be designed with the needs and values of their human users in mind. This includes prioritising transparency, explainability, and user control, as well as ensuring that AI systems are developed and deployed in a manner that respects human rights and promotes social good. The AI landscape is constantly evolving, and as such, it is essential to continually evaluate and adapt our approaches to AI development and usage. This includes monitoring the impacts of AI systems on society, updating ethical frameworks and regulatory mechanisms as needed, and remaining responsive to new challenges and opportunities that arise.

Chapter Four: Combing AI and Google Search for Your Business

The marriage of artificial intelligence (AI) and Google Search has given birth to a powerful synergy that has revolutionised the way businesses approach digital marketing and search engine optimisation (SEO). By leveraging AI, Google Search has become smarter, more efficient, and capable of providing more relevant results to users. This evolution has driven businesses to adapt and optimise their strategies, ensuring they remain competitive in an ever-changing digital landscape. Embracing the synergistic relationship between AI and Google Search is now a fundamental aspect of any successful online marketing strategy.

AI has become increasingly significant in the realm of search engine optimisation and marketing, as it enables businesses to better understand and cater to their target audience's needs. With the introduction of AI-powered algorithms, Google Search has become more adept at interpreting search intent, evaluating content quality, and generating personalised results. As a result, businesses must continually refine their SEO and content marketing efforts to stay ahead of the curve and capitalise on the opportunities presented by AI-driven search enhancements.

Moreover, AI has given rise to advanced tools and platforms that can significantly improve the efficiency and effectiveness of marketing campaigns. These innovations allow businesses to analyse massive amounts of data, gain deeper insights into customer behaviour, and make data-driven decisions to optimise their marketing strategies.

Google has been at the forefront of integrating AI technology into its search engine, enhancing its capabilities and providing users with a more accurate and personalised experience. Some of the key AI-driven features that Google has incorporated into its search engine have been mentioned in prior chapters. However, it is important to highlight the significance of these updates.

Introduced in 2015, RankBrain is an AI-powered component of Google's Search algorithm that helps process and interpret search queries, particularly those that are ambiguous or have never been seen before. RankBrain employs machine learning to understand the context and meaning behind queries, allowing it to deliver more relevant and accurate search results.

Launched in 2019, BERT is a natural language processing (NLP) model that enables Google Search to better understand the nuances of human language. By analysing the context of words in a sentence, BERT can comprehend search queries more accurately and provide more relevant results, especially for complex or conversational queries.

Passage indexing is an AI-driven feature that allows Google Search to index and rank specific passages from a web page rather than the entire page as a whole. By doing so, Google can deliver more precise results for specific questions, improving the overall user experience.

Google Lens, an AI-powered image recognition tool, allows users to search for information using images rather than text queries. This advanced technology can identify objects, landmarks, and text within images, providing relevant search results and enhancing the search experience.

These AI-driven features, among others, demonstrate Google's commitment to harnessing the power of artificial intelligence to refine and enhance its search engine capabilities, setting new standards for user experience and search engine optimisation.

AI has significantly improved the ability of search engines to understand user intent and provide more relevant results by employing natural language processing (NLP) and machine learning algorithms. These technologies allow search engines to analyse and interpret the context of search queries, taking into consideration factors like synonyms, semantics, and the relationships between words. By comprehending the nuances of human language, AI-powered search engines can better gauge the intent behind users' queries and deliver search results that closely match their needs and expectations.

AI also plays a crucial role in refining search results by tracking and analysing user behaviour and preferences. Machine learning algorithms can process vast amounts of data generated by users' search habits, clicks, and browsing patterns, enabling search engines to discern trends, preferences, and areas of interest. By understanding individual users' behaviour and preferences, AI can personalise search results, prioritising content that is likely to resonate with each user.

Furthermore, AI can identify patterns of user satisfaction or dissatisfaction based on factors like click-through rates, time spent on a page, and bounce rates. These insights enable search engines to continually refine their algorithms, ensuring that search results become increasingly relevant and useful over time.

Relevancy plays a critical role in determining the quality of search results, and AI has been instrumental in helping Google identify and prioritise the most relevant content for users. Several AI-driven techniques contribute to this process.

One such technique is semantic analysis. AI-powered algorithms can analyse the context and meaning of words within a search query, enabling Google to identify content that is semantically related and likely to address the user's query effectively. By understanding the nuances of language, AI can better match search results to the intent behind a user's query.

Another aspect of AI's contribution to relevancy is content evaluation. AI can assess the quality and relevance of content on a web page by analysing factors like readability, originality, and the presence of multimedia elements. This evaluation helps Google rank higher-quality content that is more likely to satisfy users' information needs.

AI also plays a role in link analysis. By evaluating the quality and relevance of external links pointing to a web page, AI algorithms can determine the page's authority and trustworthiness. This analysis helps Google prioritise content from reputable sources that are more likely to provide accurate and reliable information.

Lastly, AI can analyse user engagement metrics, such as click-through rates, dwell time, and bounce rates, to gauge the relevancy and usefulness of search results. These insights allow Google to continuously refine its ranking algorithms and deliver more relevant content to users.

Natural language processing (NLP) plays a vital role in enabling search engines to return more accurate query results. NLP allows search engines to analyse and understand human language, including its syntax, context, and semantics. This deep understanding of language enables search engines to better interpret search queries, particularly those that are complex or conversational in nature.

By employing NLP, search engines can discern the meaning and intent behind a user's query, even when the query contains multiple potential interpretations. This allows search engines to deliver search results that closely match users' needs and expectations, ultimately resulting in a more satisfying and accurate search experience.

Machine learning, a subset of AI, plays a crucial role in analysing user intent and improving the understanding of search queries. Machine learning algorithms are capable of processing vast amounts of data and identifying patterns, trends, and correlations within that data.

In the context of search engines, machine learning algorithms can analyse users' search patterns, clicks, and browsing behaviour, enabling search engines to discern user intent and preferences. By identifying trends and patterns in users' search habits, machine learning algorithms can make predictions about the type of content that will be most relevant and useful to individual users.

Furthermore, machine learning enables search engines to continuously refine their algorithms and improve their understanding of queries over time. As search engines process more data and receive feedback from user interactions, machine learning algorithms can adapt and evolve, ultimately resulting in more accurate and relevant search results for users.

Google has implemented AI-driven technologies to enhance various aspects of its search engine, including ranking websites, filtering spam, and identifying malicious content. These advancements contribute significantly to improving the user experience and maintaining the integrity of search results.

One prominent example is RankBrain, an AI-powered component of Google's search algorithm that helps process and understand complex search queries. RankBrain uses machine learning to analyse vast amounts of data, discern patterns, and make predictions about the most relevant content for users. By incorporating RankBrain, Google can better interpret user intent and deliver more accurate search results.

Another example is BERT (Bidirectional Encoder Representations from Transformers), an advanced AI model for natural language understanding. Google employs BERT to improve its comprehension of the nuances of human language, including context, relationships between words, and multiple meanings. By utilising BERT, Google can better understand search queries, leading to more relevant and accurate search results.

Google also uses AI to filter spam and low-quality content. AI algorithms can detect patterns and features that are characteristic of spammy or low-quality websites, such as keyword stuffing, excessive ads, or low-quality backlinks. By identifying and filtering out such content, Google ensures that users receive higher-quality search results.

In addition, AI helps Google identify and combat malicious content, such as phishing sites, malware distribution sites, and sites that exploit security vulnerabilities. AI-driven systems can analyse web content and links to identify suspicious patterns and signatures, allowing Google to remove or demote potentially harmful websites from search results. This not only improves the quality of search results but also helps protect users from online threats.

The fusion of AI and Google Search offers numerous benefits for businesses, particularly in terms of improved search engine visibility, enhanced customer targeting, and more effective marketing strategies. One of the ways businesses can capitalise on the combination of AI and Google Search is through personalised marketing. AI enables businesses to analyse user behaviour, preferences, and search history, allowing them to create targeted marketing campaigns that resonate with their audience and drive higher conversion rates.

AI also plays a significant role in search engine optimisation (SEO). By leveraging AI-driven tools and technologies, businesses can better understand user intent, optimise their website content, and develop more effective SEO strategies. For instance, AI can help businesses identify relevant keywords, analyse search trends, and generate insights that inform their content creation and optimisation efforts. This, in turn, can lead to improved search engine rankings, increased organic traffic, and, ultimately, greater online visibility.

Businesses can take advantage of AI-powered tools to streamline their keyword research and content optimisation processes. These tools utilise machine learning and natural language processing to analyse large volumes of data, identify patterns, and provide actionable insights that can help businesses enhance their online presence.

For keyword research, AI-driven tools can help businesses identify high-value keywords that are relevant to their products or services, uncover long-tail keywords with lower competition, and discover keyword trends to capitalise on. By incorporating these keywords strategically into their content, businesses can improve their search engine rankings and attract more targeted traffic.

In terms of content optimisation, AI-powered tools can analyse existing content, identify areas of improvement, and provide recommendations for optimisation. These tools can help businesses ensure that their content is relevant, engaging, and optimised for both search engines and users. By using AI-driven tools to optimise content, businesses can increase the likelihood of their content being discovered and shared, leading to improved search engine performance and greater online visibility.

Incorporating AI-driven techniques for on-page and off-page SEO can help businesses achieve better search engine rankings and drive more organic traffic. For on-page SEO, AI-powered tools can analyse a website's content, metadata, and keyword usage, providing insights and recommendations for improvement. These recommendations may include optimising title tags, meta descriptions, header tags, and keyword density, ensuring that content is relevant and engaging for users while adhering to search engine guidelines.

For off-page SEO, AI-driven tools can help businesses identify valuable backlink opportunities and assess the quality of their existing backlinks. By leveraging machine learning and data analysis, these tools can uncover patterns and trends that inform businesses' link-building strategies. This can ultimately result in a more robust backlink profile, which is a crucial factor in search engine rankings.

AI can also play a vital role in improving the technical aspects of SEO, such as site structure, speed, and crawlability. AI-driven tools can analyse a website's architecture and identify potential issues that may hinder its performance or search engine indexing. These insights can guide businesses in making improvements to their site structure, such as creating a clear hierarchy, ensuring proper internal linking, and implementing XML sitemaps.

Additionally, AI-powered tools can analyse website speed and performance, identifying factors that may be causing slowdowns or suboptimal user experiences. By addressing these issues, businesses can improve their website's loading speed, which is not only essential for user satisfaction but also a ranking factor in search engines.

Improving a site's crawlability is another area where AI can be invaluable. AI-driven tools can identify crawl errors, broken links, and other issues that may prevent search engines from properly indexing a website. By resolving these issues, businesses can ensure that their site is more easily discoverable and accessible by search engines.

An AI-driven content strategy can significantly enhance a business's online presence and performance. By leveraging AI-powered tools, businesses can analyse user preferences, search intent, and trends, which can inform their content planning and creation efforts. This enables businesses to create content that is not only engaging and relevant but also tailored to their target audience's needs and interests.

Moreover, AI-driven tools can aid in the performance analysis of a business's content strategy. These tools can provide data-driven insights into content performance, such as traffic, engagement, and conversions. By understanding which types of content resonate with their audience, businesses can refine their content strategy and make data-informed decisions to improve their overall online performance.

In today's digital landscape, user experience (UX) optimisation is crucial for attracting and retaining customers, as well as for achieving better search engine rankings. AI can significantly contribute to enhancing UX by providing data-driven insights and facilitating more personalised interactions. By focusing on AI-driven UX optimisation, businesses can create more engaging and user-friendly websites, which in turn can lead to increased conversions and customer satisfaction.

AI-powered tools can be employed to analyse website UX and provide actionable recommendations for improvement. These tools can assess various aspects of a website's design and functionality, such as navigation, layout, readability, and responsiveness. By analysing user behaviour data and employing machine learning algorithms, these tools can identify potential pain points and areas for enhancement, helping businesses create more user-friendly and intuitive websites.

AI-driven tools can facilitate A/B testing and multivariate testing, allowing businesses to experiment with different design elements and content variations. This enables businesses to determine which combinations perform best in terms of user engagement, conversions, and other key performance indicators (KPIs). By leveraging AI-powered tools for UX analysis and improvement, businesses can continuously optimise their websites and deliver a superior user experience.

AI can also be used to create personalised experiences and content recommendations for users. By analysing user behaviour, preferences, and search history, AI-driven tools can generate individualised content suggestions tailored to each user's interests and needs. This can lead to increased engagement, longer session durations, and higher conversion rates, as users are more likely to interact with content that is relevant and meaningful to them.

Measuring success is critical for businesses seeking to optimise their online presence and marketing efforts. AI and analytics tools can provide valuable insights into website and campaign performance, allowing businesses to track their progress and make data-informed decisions. By leveraging AI-driven analytics, businesses can better understand their audience, identify areas of improvement, and ultimately achieve greater success in the digital realm.

AI-driven analytics tools can provide businesses with in-depth insights into various aspects of their website and campaign performance. These tools can analyse user behaviour, traffic sources, conversion rates, and other key metrics to help businesses understand how their website is performing and where improvements can be made. Additionally, AI-powered analytics tools can evaluate campaign performance, helping businesses identify successful strategies and areas for optimisation.

AI-driven analytics can also assist businesses in tracking and optimising key performance indicators (KPIs) relevant to their specific goals and objectives. By analysing performance data, AI-powered tools can identify trends and patterns that can be used to inform decision-making and optimisation efforts. By focusing on data-driven KPIs, businesses can make informed decisions about where to allocate resources and which strategies to prioritise for maximum impact.

AI-powered predictive analytics and forecasting tools can provide valuable insights for businesses seeking to optimise their search engine marketing efforts. By analysing historical data and current trends, these tools can generate predictions about future performance, allowing businesses to make proactive decisions and adjust their strategies accordingly.

For instance, predictive analytics can help businesses identify seasonal trends, anticipate shifts in consumer behaviour, and forecast the impact of external factors on search engine performance. By leveraging AI-driven predictive analytics, businesses can stay ahead of the curve and make more informed decisions about their search engine marketing strategies, ultimately leading to improved performance and greater online success.

The integration of AI in search engines has led to a multitude of benefits that ultimately improve the quality of search results and enhance user experiences. One of the primary advantages of AI is its ability to enable search engines to deliver personalised results based on users' search history, preferences, and behaviour. This tailored approach results in a more relevant and satisfying search experience for individual users.

AI technologies, such as natural language processing and machine learning, allow search engines to better comprehend user intent behind search queries, resulting in more accurate and relevant search results. In addition, AI-powered algorithms can analyse and evaluate the quality andnrelevance of web content, ensuring that high-quality, trustworthy sources rank higher in search results.

Moreover, AI algorithms can process vast amounts of data at lightning speed, enabling search engines to return results more quickly and efficiently. This significantly contributes to a more streamlined and convenient search experience for users.

To stay competitive in the ever-evolving digital landscape, businesses must be prepared to embrace AI in their Google search strategies. This entails staying informed about AI advancements, adapting to the changing search landscape, and balancing automation with human expertise. By doing so, businesses can capitalise on the benefits of AI and position themselves for long-term success in the digital marketplace.

Keeping abreast of AI advancements and their implications for search engines is crucial for businesses looking to maintain a cutting-edge search strategy. This can involve following industry news, attending conferences, and staying connected with experts in the field. By staying informed about the latest developments in AI, businesses can better understand how these technologies are shaping the search landscape and how they can be leveraged to enhance their search engine marketing efforts.

As the search landscape evolves, businesses must be prepared to adapt their strategies and integrate AI-driven tools into their workflows. This can include implementing AI-powered SEO tools, analytics platforms, and content optimisation solutions. By embracing AI-driven technologies, businesses can optimise their search strategies, streamline processes, and ultimately achieve better results in terms of search engine rankings, traffic, and conversions.

While AI-driven tools can offer significant benefits in terms of efficiency and performance, it's essential to strike the right balance between automation and human expertise in your search engine marketing approach. Human expertise remains critical for interpreting data, understanding context, and making strategic decisions based on AI-generated insights.

By integrating AI-driven tools with the knowledge and experience of marketing professionals, businesses can create a more comprehensive and effective search engine marketing strategy that leverages the best of both worlds. This approach can enable businesses to stay agile, adapt to changing search engine dynamics, and maintain a competitive edge in the digital marketplace.

Human involvement is essential for ensuring that AI systems operate effectively and ethically. One of the key benefits of human involvement in AI is the contextual understanding that humans possess. They have a deep understanding of context, culture, and nuance, which AI systems may struggle to replicate. Human input can help guide AI systems in making better decisions, particularly in complex or sensitive situations.

Another advantage of human involvement in AI is creativity and innovation. While AI systems can analyse data and identify patterns, human creativity is still vital for generating new ideas, exploring uncharted territories, and finding innovative solutions to complex problems. As AI continues to advance, there is growing concern about its impact on human labour. While AI has the potential to automate certain tasks and improve efficiency, it may also lead to job displacement in some industries. However, it is important to recognise that AI can also create new job opportunities by giving rise to new industries and requiring new skill sets.

To mitigate potential negative impacts on human labour, businesses and governments should invest in workforce development, reskilling, and education initiatives to prepare individuals for the jobs of the future. By doing so, society can ensure that people have the necessary skills to adapt and thrive in an AI-driven world.

The use of AI to replace human workers raises several ethical considerations. For instance, businesses must weigh the benefits of increased efficiency and cost savings against potential job losses and the subsequent impact on employees and communities. There are also concerns about the potential loss of human touch in certain industries, particularly in fields like healthcare, education, and customer service, where empathy and human connection are integral to the quality of service.

To address these ethical concerns, businesses should carefully assess the potential consequences of AI adoption and consider implementing policies that prioritise responsible and inclusive AI deployment. This may include investing in workforce development, promoting the responsible use of AI in decision-making, and ensuring that human oversight remains a key component of AI-driven processes. By taking a thoughtful and ethical approach to AI adoption, businesses can balance the benefits of automation with the need to protect human interests and values.

The accuracy of AI systems, when compared to humans, varies depending on the task at hand. In some areas, AI has proven to be more accurate than human judgement, such as in pattern recognition, data analysis, and complex calculations. However, AI systems may struggle with tasks that require a deep understanding of context, emotion, or cultural nuance, where human intuition and empathy are critical.

In order to achieve the best results, it is essential to recognise the strengths and limitations of AI systems and to combine them with human expertise when necessary. This collaborative approach can lead to more accurate and effective outcomes in various applications.

The question of whether machines should be held responsible for their actions is a complex and ongoing debate. As AI systems become more autonomous, it becomes increasingly difficult to attribute responsibility to a single entity, be it a human or a machine. Legal and ethical frameworks will need to evolve to address this challenge and to ensure that AI systems are developed and deployed in a responsible and accountable manner.

One potential solution is to establish clear guidelines and standards for AI development, focusing on transparency, explainability, and human oversight. This can help ensure that AI systems are designed with ethical considerations in mind and that any negative consequences can be traced back to human decision-makers or developers.

AI integration into everyday life offers numerous advantages, such as increased efficiency, personalised experiences, and improved decision-making. However, there are also potential disadvantages, including privacy concerns, digital dependency, and the potential loss of human touch in certain interactions. To strike the right balance, it is crucial for businesses, governments, and individuals to be aware of these trade-offs and to adopt a responsible approach to AI implementation. By doing so, society can harness the benefits of AI while minimising its potential drawbacks.

In the workplace, AI offers advantages such as increased productivity, cost savings, and improved decision-making.

However, there are also potential disadvantages, including job displacement, a need for reskilling, and concerns about employee surveillance and data privacy.

To navigate these challenges, businesses should prioritise workforce development, transparency, and employee well-being when integrating AI into their operations. This will help ensure that the transition to AI-driven processes is smooth, equitable, and beneficial for all stakeholders involved.

Excessive reliance on AI can lead to several challenges, such as overdependence on technology, reduced human interaction, and ethical concerns. Over-reliance on AI can result in a loss of critical thinking skills and the ability to adapt to novel situations. Additionally, there are potential risks associated with AI biases, security vulnerabilities, and the misuse of AI for malicious purposes.

To mitigate these challenges, it is essential for businesses and individuals to maintain a healthy balance between AI-driven processes and human expertise. By adopting a responsible and balanced approach to AI integration, society can enjoy the benefits of AI while minimising potential risks and challenges.

Chapter Five: AI and Content Marketing

As the digital landscape continues to evolve, content marketing remains a critical component of successful marketing strategies. In this competitive environment, businesses are increasingly turning to artificial intelligence (AI) to enhance their content marketing efforts. The integration of AI-driven tools and techniques into content creation, distribution, and optimisation has the potential to revolutionise the way businesses engage with their target audience and deliver value to their customers.

In this chapter, we will explore the significance of AI in the content marketing landscape and discuss the transformative potential of AI-driven tools to enhance various aspects of content marketing. By understanding how AI can be effectively integrated into content marketing strategies, businesses can leverage these advanced technologies to create more engaging, relevant, and impactful content that resonates with their audience and drives sustainable growth.

The rising role of AI in content marketing is fueled by several factors, including the increasing availability of advanced algorithms, the growing volume of data available for analysis, and the need for businesses to differentiate themselves in an increasingly competitive marketplace. AI-driven tools have the power to help marketers better understand their audience, create more compelling content, and optimise their strategies for maximum impact. As we delve deeper into the various aspects of AI and content marketing in the following sections, we will discover how businesses can harness the power of AI to revolutionise their content marketing efforts and create a more efficient, personalised, and connected experience for their customers.

One of the most significant ways AI is transforming content marketing is through the emergence of AI-driven content generation tools and platforms. These cutting-edge technologies have the potential to not only streamline the content creation process but also to improve the quality and relevance of the content produced. By leveraging advanced algorithms and natural language processing (NLP) capabilities, AI-powered content generation tools can help marketers create content faster and more efficiently while maintaining high standards of quality and accuracy.

To effectively leverage AI-generated content in marketing strategies, it is crucial to understand the capabilities and limitations of these tools. While AI-driven content generation platforms can produce coherent and grammatically correct content, they may not always convey the nuances and subtleties of human language or capture the unique brand voice of a business. Therefore, it is important for marketers to strike a balance between human creativity and AI-driven automation. In practice, this often involves using AI-generated content as a starting point or draft, which can then be refined, edited, and customised by human writers to ensure it aligns with the brand identity and messaging.

Another key aspect of using AI-powered content generation tools effectively is selecting the right platform or tool for the specific needs of a business. There are a variety of AI-driven content generation solutions available in the market, each with its unique features, capabilities, and use cases. For example, some tools are designed to create short-form content like social media posts and ad copy, while others excel at generating long-form content like blog articles and whitepapers. By carefully evaluating and selecting the most suitable tool for their content marketing needs, businesses can maximise the benefits of AI-driven content generation and drive better results from their content marketing efforts.

There are several AI-driven tools available for creating content that is engaging, relevant, and optimised for search engines. One popular option is OpenAI's GPT-3, a state-of-the-art language model capable of generating human-like text based on a given input. This model can be employed for various content creation tasks, such as writing articles and generating social media posts.

Another tool is Copy.ai, an AI-powered copywriting tool that uses GPT-3 to generate content for multiple purposes, including blog posts, product descriptions, social media updates, and email templates. MarketMuse is an AI-driven content optimisation platform providing insights on keyword research, content structure, and competitive analysis. It can help you create content optimised for search engines and tailored to your target audience's needs.

Frase.io is an AI-powered content creation and optimisation tool that offers keyword suggestions, content briefs, and optimisation recommendations based on real time search data. WordAi is an AI-driven article spinner and rewriter that can help you generate unique and readable content from existing articles or blog posts.

These tools can significantly enhance your content creation process by automating various tasks, generating insights, and optimising your content for search engines and user engagement. By leveraging these AI-driven tools, you can create high-quality, relevant content that effectively resonates with your target audience. With AI, the possibilities are endless, and you are bound to find software for every purpose of your campaign.

Incorporating AI into the content creation process can significantly enhance the quality, efficiency, and effectiveness of content marketing efforts. Below, we will discuss practical steps for leveraging AI-driven tools to write content that is engaging, relevant, and tailored to the needs of the target audience.

1. Choose the right AI-driven content generation tool: Before you begin, it is essential to select an AI content generation platform or tool that aligns with your specific content marketing needs. Evaluate various tools based on their capabilities, the quality of content they produce, and their ease of use. Consider factors such as the types of content the tool can generate (e.g., short-form versus long-form) and its ability to understand and adapt to your brand's voice and tone.

2. Define your content goals and target audience: Before generating content with AI, clearly outline the purpose of the content, the intended audience, and the key messages you want to convey. Having a clear understanding of these elements will help you guide the AI tool in creating content that aligns with your marketing objectives and resonates with your target audience.

3. Generate an outline or draft with AI: Utilise the AI content generation tool to create an initial draft or outline of your content. This may involve inputting a series of keywords, a topic, or a brief description of the content you want to produce. The AI tool will then generate content based on these inputs, which can be a starting point for further refinement and editing.

4. Refine and edit the AI-generated content: While AI-driven tools can generate coherent and relevant content, human intervention is often required to ensure that the content is of high quality and aligns

with your brand's voice and messaging. Edit the AI-generated content to address any inconsistencies, grammatical errors, or content gaps. This step may involve refining the language, adding personal anecdotes or examples, and incorporating your unique perspective and expertise to make the content more engaging and informative.

5. Optimise content for SEO and user experience: Once you have refined and edited the AI-generated content, optimise it for search engines and user experience. This may include incorporating relevant keywords, adding meta tags and titles, optimising headings and subheadings, and ensuring that the content is easily scannable and accessible to readers.

6. Monitor content performance and refine your strategy: Finally, use AI-driven analytics tools to monitor the performance of your AI-generated content. By analysing metrics such as engagement, conversions, and audience behaviour, you can gain insights into the effectiveness of your content marketing efforts and make data-driven decisions to refine your strategy and improve future content.

In addition to content generation, AI is also revolutionising how businesses analyse and strategise their content marketing efforts. By harnessing the power of AI-powered analytics, marketers can gather actionable insights on content performance, audience engagement, and consumer preferences, which can help them make data-driven decisions and optimise their strategies accordingly.

One of the key advantages of AI-driven analytics is the ability to process vast amounts of data in real time, allowing marketers to understand the impact of their content on their target audience more effectively. Through advanced algorithms and machine learning techniques, AI-powered tools can identify patterns and trends that may not be immediately apparent to human analysts, helping marketers to uncover valuable insights that can drive their content strategies.

By leveraging AI for audience segmentation and persona development, businesses can create more personalised and relevant content that resonates with their target audience. AI-driven analytics can analyse demographic, behavioural, and psychographic data to create detailed audience personas, which can be used to guide content creation and messaging. This level of personalisation enables businesses to engage with their audience on a deeper level, fostering stronger relationships and driving better results from their content marketing efforts.

Another way AI can help businesses refine their content strategies is through AI-generated recommendations and insights. By analysing content performance data, AI-driven tools can suggest topics, formats, and distribution channels that are likely to generate the highest engagement and conversions. By incorporating these recommendations into their content marketing strategies, businesses can optimise their efforts and focus on producing content that delivers maximum value to their audience.

Effectively distributing and promoting content is critical to the success of any content marketing campaign. AI-driven technologies offer a powerful solution for optimising content distribution and promotion efforts, ensuring that your content reaches the right audience at the right time and through the most appropriate channels.

AI-powered tools can analyse vast amounts of audience data, identifying patterns and preferences that can inform your content distribution strategy. By understanding which channels and platforms are most effective in engaging your target audience, you can prioritise and allocate resources more efficiently, ensuring that your content reaches the largest and most receptive audience possible. Additionally, AI can help you determine the optimal times for publishing and sharing content, maximising its visibility and impact.

In the realm of social media management and content promotion, AI-driven tools offer a myriad of benefits. These tools can automate content scheduling and posting, saving time and resources while ensuring a consistent online presence. They can also analyse social media performance data, providing insights into the types of content that resonate most with your audience and generating recommendations for improving engagement and reach. Some AI-driven tools even offer features like predictive analytics and sentiment analysis, which can help you fine-tune your content and promotional strategies to better connect with your audience.

One of the key advantages of using AI for content distribution and promotion is the ability to ensure consistent brand messaging and targeting across diverse channels. With AI-driven tools, businesses can effectively manage their brand voice, style, and tone, creating a cohesive and engaging content experience for their audience. This consistency is essential for building brand recognition, trust, and loyalty among consumers.

Moreover, AI-driven tools can help marketers adapt their content promotion efforts to the ever-changing digital landscape, identifying new platforms and channels as they emerge and gauging their potential impact on content engagement. This adaptability allows businesses to stay ahead of the curve and capitalise on emerging trends and opportunities in the digital marketing space.

In today's digital landscape, content optimisation and search engine optimisation (SEO) play crucial roles in ensuring that your content is visible and easily discoverable by your target audience. AI-driven technologies have emerged as powerful tools to assist in keyword research, SEO optimisation, and adapting to the evolving role of AI in search engine algorithms.

AI-powered tools have the ability to process and analyse large amounts of data quickly, making them particularly valuable for keyword research and SEO optimisation. By sifting through vast datasets, these tools can identify high-performing keywords and phrases, as well as provide insights into search intent, trends, and user behaviour. This enables content creators to develop content that is not only engaging and relevant to their audience but also optimised for search engine visibility.

Maximising content visibility and engagement go hand in hand with employing AI-driven SEO techniques. AI-powered tools can provide real time feedback and recommendations on content optimisation, ensuring that your content is structured and formatted to maximise its discoverability and performance in search engine rankings. Moreover, these tools can help you stay abreast of the latest SEO best practices, enabling you to adapt your content and optimise strategies as search engine algorithms evolve.

The role of AI in search engine algorithms is becoming increasingly prominent as search engines strive to deliver more accurate and personalised results for users. AI-driven technologies, such as natural language processing and machine learning, enable search engines to understand the content and context of web pages better, resulting in more relevant search results for users. As a content marketer, it is essential to be aware of the evolving role of AI in search engine algorithms and adapt your content optimisation and SEO strategies accordingly.

As AI-driven technologies continue to transform the world of content marketing, it is essential for marketers and content creators to balance the benefits of these advancements with the ethical considerations that arise. Navigating issues related to authenticity, transparency, and accountability is crucial in maintaining the trust of your audience and fostering a responsible content marketing landscape.

Authenticity is a vital aspect of content marketing, as it helps build trust and credibility with your audience. In the context of AI-driven content marketing, ensuring authenticity may involve being transparent about the use of AI-generated content or disclosing the role of AI in content creation. By openly communicating the role of AI in your content marketing efforts, you can mitigate potential concerns surrounding authenticity and maintain a genuine connection with your audience.

Transparency and accountability are closely related to the issue of authenticity. As AI-driven tools become more sophisticated, it becomes increasingly important for marketers to be transparent about their use of these technologies and the extent to which they influence content creation and promotion. This transparency allows audiences to make informed decisions about the content they consume while also fostering an environment of accountability where content creators are held responsible for the accuracy and ethics of their AI-generated content.

Addressing potential ethical concerns associated with AI-generated content is critical to developing responsible content marketing practices. This may involve establishing guidelines and best practices for the ethical use of AI-driven tools in content creation, ensuring that AI-generated content does not promote misinformation, perpetuate biases, or infringe on intellectual property rights. By proactively addressing these concerns, marketers can build trust with their audience and pave the way for the responsible use of AI in content marketing.

As AI continues to evolve and reshape the content marketing landscape, it is crucial for marketers and content creators to be prepared for the future of AI-driven content marketing. This involves anticipating emerging trends and innovations, adapting to changes in consumer behaviour, technology, and industry standards, and fostering a culture of continuous learning and innovation within your organisation.

Staying ahead of emerging trends and innovations in AI-driven content marketing requires staying informed about advancements in the field and regularly monitoring new developments. By staying up-to-date on the latest research, tools, and platforms, you can better understand the capabilities and limitations of AI in content marketing, enabling you to make informed decisions and take advantage of new opportunities.

Adapting to changes in consumer behaviour, technology, and industry standards is essential for staying competitive in the rapidly evolving digital landscape. As AI-driven technologies become more sophisticated, consumer expectations and behaviours may shift, requiring content creators and marketers to adjust their strategies accordingly. By closely monitoring these changes, marketers can ensure their content remains relevant, engaging, and effective in achieving their objectives.

Fostering a culture of continuous learning and innovation within your organisation is key to staying agile in the face of rapid technological advancements. Encourage employees to pursue professional development opportunities and embrace new technologies as they become available. This commitment to learning and growth will empower your team to stay at the forefront of AI-driven content marketing, maximising your chances of success in this fast-paced and ever-changing field.

As we have seen throughout this chapter, integrating AI-driven tools and techniques into content marketing strategies is essential and offers a wealth of business opportunities. By harnessing the power of AI, content marketers can unlock new levels of growth, innovation, and competitive advantage, ultimately resulting in sustainable success in an increasingly digital world.

The importance of incorporating AI into content marketing strategies cannot be overstated. AI-driven technologies enable marketers to better understand their audience, streamline content creation, enhance content distribution and promotion, and optimise content for search engines. By leveraging these capabilities, businesses can deliver more targeted, engaging, and effective content, leading to improved customer relationships, higher conversion rates, and, ultimately, greater ROI.

The potential of AI to drive growth and innovation in content marketing is vast, and businesses that are willing to explore and embrace this transformative technology are likely to gain a significant competitive advantage. By staying informed about the latest advancements and continuously learning and adapting, content marketers can make the most of AI-driven tools and techniques, ensuring their strategies remain cutting-edge and their businesses stay ahead of the curve.

Chapter Six: The Impact of Voice Search and Virtual Assistants

In recent years, voice search and virtual assistants have emerged as game-changing technologies, transforming how users interact with their devices and access information. Voice-enabled devices, such as smart speakers and smartphones, have become increasingly common in households and workplaces across the globe, reflecting a broader shift in search behaviour. The development of voice search and virtual assistants has revolutionised how people interact with technology and access information. Voice-enabled devices such as smart speakers, smartphones, and wearables have rapidly become integral to daily life and are transforming search behaviour.

The technology behind voice search uses natural language processing (NLP) to interpret the context of a query and generate relevant search results. This means that users can conduct searches without having to type, providing a more effortless and convenient search experience. Virtual assistants, such as Amazon's Alexa or Google Assistant, offer more than just answers to queries and can perform a variety of tasks, such as playing music, setting reminders, or even controlling smart home devices.

The proliferation of voice-enabled devices like Amazon Echo, Google Home, and Apple HomePod has led to a significant change in the way people search for information. As voice recognition technology continues to improve, more and more users are turning to voice search for its convenience, speed, and ease of use. This transition has prompted businesses and marketers to rethink their approach to search engine optimisation and content creation, as traditional text-based strategies may not be as effective in catering to voice search queries. According to a survey by Adobe, 48% of consumers use voice assistants for general web searches, while 31% use them to search for products or services.

Voice search has been particularly popular among younger demographics, with technology becoming the primary search method for Generation Z and Millennials. This has implications for businesses looking to reach these audiences, as voice search can significantly impact how users discover and engage with their brand.

The growing adoption of voice search has also impacted user behaviour. Searches conducted through voice tend to be more conversational and question-based, as users naturally speak in longer, more complex sentences than they would type. This shift in search behaviour necessitates give us a more nuanced understanding of user intent, as businesses must be able to provide relevant, accurate, and easily digestible information in response to voice queries.

As voice search becomes increasingly prevalent, businesses must adapt to ensure they remain visible and competitive in this evolving landscape. Voice search optimisation is quickly becoming a critical aspect of digital marketing, as traditional SEO tactics may not be sufficient for capturing voice search traffic. Businesses need to develop strategies that cater specifically to voice queries, focusing on long-tail keywords, natural language, and question-based content.

In addition to optimising their online presence for voice search, businesses must also consider the role of virtual assistants in shaping the user experience. Virtual assistants like Siri, Alexa, and Google Assistant are rapidly becoming an integral part of users' daily lives, assisting with tasks ranging from setting reminders to making purchases. By understanding the unique capabilities and limitations of these virtual assistants, businesses can better leverage their potential and create seamless, engaging experiences for users.

Artificial intelligence (AI) plays a crucial role in the development of voice search and virtual assistant technology. AI helps voice assistants understand and interpret spoken language, making it possible for them to recognise user requests and respond appropriately. One of the key ways AI is used in voice search and virtual assistant development is through machine learning. Machine learning is a type of AI that enables systems to learn and improve over time through data analysis. Voice assistants use machine learning algorithms to analyse large datasets of speech and language patterns, allowing them to improve their accuracy and effectiveness over time.

Another important use of AI in voice search and virtual assistant development is in the creation of personalised experiences for users. By analysing user data, AI can help voice assistants learn about individual preferences and behaviours, allowing them to provide more relevant and tailored responses to user requests.

As AI technology continues to advance, it is likely that voice search and virtual assistants will become even more sophisticated and intuitive. AI will play a crucial role in making these systems more accurate, efficient, and capable of understanding and responding to user needs in real time.

As the popularity of the use of voice search and virtual assistants continues to grow, it is becoming increasingly important for businesses to understand the underlying technology that powers these systems. By gaining a deeper understanding of how voice search works, businesses can better optimise their online presence and create experiences that cater to the needs of their customers.

When a user speaks into a device with voice search capabilities, the words are first captured by a microphone and then processed by a speech recognition algorithm. This algorithm then converts the speech into text that can be analysed by an NLP system. The NLP system then uses a combination of language modelling, text analysis, and machine learning algorithms to identify the intent behind the spoken words.

The system can then use this intent to return relevant search results, perform actions, or provide answers to the user's query. NLP also enables voice assistants to respond to follow-up questions or requests, creating a more natural and conversational experience for the user. As voice search technology continues to evolve and improve, NLP will play an increasingly important role in making these systems more accurate, efficient, and effective.

Virtual assistants have become an integral part of modern society, providing users with quick and convenient access to information through voice-based interactions. These intelligent software applications use natural language processing and machine learning algorithms to understand user requests and provide relevant responses.

Virtual assistants have a range of applications, from simple tasks like setting reminders and checking the weather, to more complex tasks like booking travel arrangements and managing finances. One of the key benefits of virtual assistants is their ability to retrieve information quickly and efficiently, making them a valuable tool for businesses and individuals alike.

Through their use of AI-powered natural language processing, virtual assistants are able to understand complex queries and provide accurate and relevant responses. They can access a wide range of information sources, from web searches and social media to local business listings and e-commerce platforms, making them a valuable resource for information retrieval.

In addition to their role in information retrieval, virtual assistants can also provide users with personalised recommendations and insights based on their individual preferences and behaviour patterns. By analysing user data and learning from past interactions, virtual assistants can provide tailored responses and suggestions, making them an increasingly valuable tool for businesses looking to personalise their customer experience.

As the use of virtual assistants continues to grow, their role in information retrieval and personalised experiences is likely to become even more important. With advances in AI and natural language processing, virtual assistants will become even more accurate and effective, providing users with an unparalleled level of convenience and efficiency.

An example of a virtual assistant includes Google Assistant. Google Assistant is one of the most popular virtual assistants, available on various devices, from smartphones to smart home devices. It is known for its accurate and fast responses, as well as its ability to integrate with a wide range of third-party apps and services. Google Assistant also has a range of voice commands that can be used to control smart home devices and perform tasks like sending messages and setting reminders.

Siri, Apple's virtual assistant, is available on iPhones, iPads, and Mac computers. It is known for its ability to perform a wide range of tasks, from setting reminders and making phone calls to booking restaurant reservations and providing directions. Siri can also be used to control smart home devices and interact with third-party apps.

Alexa, Amazon's virtual assistant, is available on the popular Echo line of smart speakers as well as a range of other devices. It is known for its ability to integrate with a wide range of smart home devices and services, making it a popular choice for home automation. Alexa can also perform a wide range of tasks, from playing music and answering trivia questions to making phone calls and placing orders on amazon.

Cortana, Microsoft's virtual assistant, is available on Windows devices and can be used to perform a range of tasks, from setting reminders and sending emails to making phone calls and providing directions. Cortana also has a range of integrations with third-party services and can be used to control smart home devices.

Each of these virtual assistants has its own unique capabilities and strengths, making them well-suited for different tasks and user preferences. As the market for virtual assistants continues to grow, it will be interesting to see how they evolve and improve to meet the changing needs of users. Virtual assistants use a combination of natural language processing (NLP) and machine learning (ML) algorithms to process and respond to voice queries. When a user speaks a voice query to a virtual assistant, the audio is first recorded and sent to the cloud for processing.

The first step in processing a voice query is to convert the audio into a digital format that can be analysed by the virtual assistant's algorithms. This is known as speech recognition, and it involves breaking the audio into individual sounds and matching them to known phonemes in the language being spoken. Once the audio has been converted into text, the virtual assistant's NLP algorithms analyse the text to identify the user's intent and extract the key information needed to respond to the query. This involves understanding the meaning behind the words and phrases used in the query, as well as identifying any context that may be relevant to the user's request.

After the user's intent has been identified, the virtual assistant uses machine learning algorithms to search through its knowledge base and find the most appropriate response to the query. This can involve accessing data from third-party services, such as weather or traffic information, or using pre-programmed responses to common questions.

Once the virtual assistant has identified the most appropriate response, it uses text-to-speech technology to convert the response back into an audio format that can be played for the user. The response is then sent back to the user's device and played through the device's speakers.

Overall, the process of processing and responding to voice queries involves a combination of sophisticated algorithms and technologies, including speech recognition, natural language processing, machine learning, and text-to-speech synthesis. As these technologies continue to improve, virtual assistants will become even more capable of understanding and responding to user queries in natural, intuitive ways.

One important consideration is the use of long-tail keywords. When using voice search, people are more likely to use natural, conversational language when making queries. This means that long-tail keywords, which are more specific and typically contain more words, are becoming increasingly important for SEO. By targeting long-tail keywords, you can improve the relevance of your content to voice search queries and increase the chances of appearing in search results.

One of the most significant factors is creating conversational and contextually relevant content. When users interact with virtual assistants, they are more likely to use natural, conversational language instead of the specific keywords or phrases they might type into a search engine. Therefore, it is essential to craft content that answers common voice search queries in a conversational and easy-to-understand manner.

Another strategy is to focus on providing direct, succinct answers to commonly asked questions related to your business or industry. This can involve creating FAQ pages or adding structured data markup to your website to make it easier for search engines to understand and display your content in response to voice queries.

It's also important to ensure that your website is mobile-friendly, as many voice searches are conducted on mobile devices. This means using responsive design and optimising page load times to provide a seamless experience for users. Ensure that your website is structured in a way that makes it easy for search engines to understand and crawl. This means using structured data markup, such as Schema.org, to provide additional context and information about your website and content.

Finally, it's important to stay up to date with the latest voice search trends and technologies. As virtual assistants and voice search continue to evolve, it's important to adapt your website and SEO strategies accordingly to ensure that your business stays ahead of the curve.

Measuring the performance of voice search and virtual assistant technology requires a different approach than traditional search engine optimisation (SEO). To understand how users are interacting with voice search and virtual assistants, businesses need to track and analyse usage data. This includes data on the types of queries being made, the frequency of voice searches, and the devices being used to access virtual assistants. By understanding how users interact with this technology, businesses can adjust their strategies to better meet their needs.

To measure the effectiveness of their voice search and virtual assistant strategies, businesses need to identify key performance indicators (KPIs). These KPIs can include metrics such as the number of voice search impressions, the number of conversions resulting from voice search queries, and the overall impact on business performance. By tracking these KPIs over time, businesses can determine the effectiveness of their voice search and virtual assistant strategies and make adjustments as needed.

AI Voice search can also impact local SEO. Local SEO is the practice of optimising a website's online presence to rank higher in local search results. Voice search is revolutionising local SEO, as more people are using voice search to find local businesses and services. By optimising your website for voice search, you can improve your visibility in local search results, attract more local customers, and ultimately grow your business. An example of this in practice is by optimising GMB listings for voice search. By doing this, businesses can improve their chances of being featured in the "local pack," which is the list of businesses that appear at the top of the search results for local queries.

It is as important to use voice search AI in your SEO strategy as it is in day-to-day business life. As virtual assistants become increasingly integrated into our daily lives, businesses are recognising the opportunities they present for reaching and engaging with customers in new ways. From answering customer queries to providing personalised recommendations, virtual assistants can help businesses provide a more efficient and tailored customer experience.

As virtual assistants become increasingly popular and more sophisticated, businesses can benefit from incorporating them into their customer support and sales processes. Virtual assistants can help businesses provide faster and more personalised customer service, leading to increased customer satisfaction and loyalty. For example, a virtual assistant can be programmed to answer frequently asked questions, offer product recommendations, and even complete purchases for customers. This can help businesses save time and resources while improving the customer experience. Virtual assistants can also be used to streamline sales processes. They can be programmed to identify potential customers, provide product information and pricing, and even schedule appointments or demos. This can help businesses save time and resources while improving their sales performance.

Virtual assistants provide an opportunity for businesses to develop custom voice apps or skills, also known as actions. These voice apps can be designed to perform a wide range of tasks, such as answering customer questions, providing product information, and even completing transactions. For example, a restaurant could develop a voice app that allows customers to place orders through a virtual assistant. Similarly, a retailer could develop a voice app that provides customers with real time inventory information and helps them find products in-store.

Developing custom voice apps requires a strong understanding of natural language processing and user behaviour. However, the potential benefits of such apps are significant, as they can provide businesses with a new way to engage with customers and streamline their operations. Virtual assistants can also be used to improve internal business operations and productivity. For example, a virtual assistant can be programmed to schedule meetings, set reminders, and even provide updates on business performance metrics.

Virtual assistants can also be used to automate routine tasks, freeing up time and resources for employees to focus on more complex and strategic initiatives. For example, a virtual assistant could be used to process employee time-off requests, eliminating the need for manual processing and reducing the likelihood of errors.

Overall, virtual assistants have the potential to significantly improve business efficiency and productivity. As their capabilities continue to expand, businesses should explore how they can best leverage this technology to support their internal operations.

As with any technology, voice search is constantly evolving and advancing. It's important for businesses to stay informed and anticipate developments and trends in order to remain competitive in their industries. One key trend is the increasing accuracy and reliability of voice recognition technology, which is leading to more sophisticated and personalised experiences for users. Another trend is the integration of voice search with other technologies, such as smart home devices and wearables, which is expanding the reach and accessibility of voice search.

With the growing importance of voice search and virtual assistants, it's essential for businesses to integrate this technology into their long-term digital marketing strategies. This means developing content that is optimised for voice search queries, such as conversational and contextually relevant content. It also involves optimising Google My Business listings and creating location-specific content for local SEO. Additionally, businesses can develop voice apps (skills/actions) for virtual assistant platforms to provide a more personalised and interactive experience for users.

As the search landscape continues to evolve and shift towards voice-enabled devices, it's important for businesses to adapt and stay ahead of the curve. This involves ensuring that websites and digital content are optimised for voice search queries and that they are accessible and compatible with voice-enabled devices. It also means staying up to date on the latest trends and developments in voice search technology and adapting strategies accordingly.

As technology continues to evolve, so does the way people search for information. The emergence of voice search and virtual assistants has brought about a significant shift in the way people interact with search engines and access information. As a result, businesses must adapt to the changing landscape in order to remain competitive and relevant in their respective industries.

In this chapter, we have explored the growing impact of voice search and virtual assistants, as well as the role of AI in their development. We have also discussed the various ways in which businesses can optimise their website and content for voice search and leverage virtual assistants to enhance their customer support, sales processes, and internal operations.

Additionally, we have covered the importance of tracking and measuring voice search performance metrics and adapting to changes in user behaviour and technology advancements. By doing so, businesses can stay ahead of the curve and maintain a competitive edge in the increasingly voice-driven search environment.

Embracing voice search and virtual assistants is crucial for businesses seeking to achieve long-term success in the digital landscape. By understanding the implications of this technology and staying up-to-date with developments and trends, businesses can remain relevant and stay ahead of the competition.

Chapter Seven: AI and Search Engine Marketing (SEM) Beyond Google

As the digital marketing landscape undergoes continuous metamorphosis, it is of paramount importance for businesses to acknowledge the necessity of diversifying their Search Engine Marketing (SEM) strategies beyond the confines of Google. While Google unquestionably maintains its hegemony in the search engine market, other platforms present distinctive opportunities for businesses to broaden their reach and engage with previously untapped audiences.

Search engine marketing (SEM) is a form of digital marketing that involves the promotion of websites and their products or services through search engine results pages (SERPs). It encompasses various techniques and strategies aimed at increasing website visibility and driving traffic from search engines. SEM includes both paid advertising and organic search optimisation, and it has become an essential component of digital marketing for businesses of all sizes.

One of the primary goals of SEM is to achieve a higher ranking on SERPs, particularly on the first page. This can be achieved through the use of paid advertising, such as pay-per-click (PPC) campaigns, or by optimising the website for relevant search queries through search engine optimisation (SEO). Paid advertising is a way of buying advertising space on the search engine results pages, whereas SEO is a way of improving the website's visibility organically by optimising the content, meta descriptions, and other technical aspects of the website.

The world of search engine marketing (SEM) extends beyond Google, and it is essential for businesses to recognise the role of other search engines and platforms in their digital marketing strategies. While Google remains the dominant player in the search engine space, it is important to also consider the search behaviours of users on other platforms such as Bing, Yahoo, and DuckDuckGo, as well as social media platforms like Facebook, Instagram, and Twitter.

While Google continues to dominate the search engine market with an 87% market share, it is important for businesses to recognise the role of other search engines and platforms in digital marketing. Bing, for example, has a growing market share of 6.61% and is the default search engine for Microsoft devices. Yahoo, despite a decline in market share, still has a significant user base and can be an important platform for specific industries.

Social media platforms such as Facebook, Instagram, and Twitter offer businesses the opportunity to target specific demographics and engage with their audience in a more interactive manner. While these platforms may not function in the same way as traditional search engines, they should be considered an important part of any comprehensive SEM strategy.

While Google is undoubtedly the dominant player in the search engine market, businesses need to consider the advantages of a diverse SEM strategy encompassing other search engines and platforms. Diversification can reduce the risks associated with relying solely on one platform and can open up new opportunities for businesses to reach their target audience.

For example, Bing Ads may offer a lower cost per click (CPC) than Google Ads for certain industries, making it an attractive option for businesses looking to maximise their return on investment. On the other hand, social media platforms offer a unique opportunity to engage with users on a more personal level and can be an effective way to build brand awareness.

Bing Ads is Microsoft's advertising platform that allows businesses to advertise on Bing Search and other Microsoft-owned platforms. Bing Ads employs AI algorithms to help advertisers create more effective campaigns and reach their target audience more efficiently. Bing Ads' AI-powered intelligent audience targeting feature helps advertisers reach the most relevant audience for their campaigns by analysing user search queries, demographics, and device types. Bing Ads' AI-powered bidding strategies also help advertisers optimise their ad spend by automatically adjusting bids based on the likelihood of conversions.

Bing may not have the same market share as Google, but it still has a significant presence in the search engine market. Bing currently holds around 6% of the global search engine market share, which translates to millions of users who could potentially be reached through SEM strategies. Bing's partnership with Yahoo also expands its reach, making it a valuable platform for businesses to consider when developing their SEM strategies. Additionally, Bing's AI capabilities allow businesses to target their audience more effectively, making it a valuable tool for businesses looking to optimise their search campaigns.

Bing Ads offers several AI-driven features and tools that advertisers can leverage to improve their SEM campaigns. One such feature is Bing's AI-powered intelligent audience targeting, which uses machine learning algorithms to analyse user search queries, demographics, and device types to identify the most relevant audience for an advertiser's campaign. Bing Ads' AI-powered bidding strategies automatically adjust bids based on the likelihood of conversions, helping advertisers optimise their ad spend. Bing's AI-powered visual search allows advertisers to promote their products visually, making it easier for users to find what they're looking for. Additionally, Bing Ads offers AI-powered ad extensions that help advertisers improve the visibility and relevancy of their ads.

To optimise their Bing Ads campaigns with AI, businesses need to understand how to leverage Bing's AI capabilities effectively. One strategy is to use Bing's AI-powered intelligent audience targeting to identify the most relevant audience for their campaigns. This can be achieved by analysing user search queries, demographics, and device types to ensure that ads are targeted to the right audience. Another strategy is to use Bing's AI-powered bidding strategies to optimise ad spend. By automatically adjusting bids based on the likelihood of conversions, businesses can achieve better ad placement and ROI. Using Bing's AI-powered visual search and ad extensions can also help businesses improve the visibility and relevancy of their ads, leading to higher click-through rates and conversions.

As the second most popular search engine globally, YouTube serves as a valuable platform for businesses to reach their target audience. YouTube's AI-powered video recommendations algorithm helps businesses improve their reach by suggesting videos to users based on their viewing history and engagement patterns. Additionally, YouTube's AI-powered targeting capabilities allow businesses to target their audience based on their demographics, interests, and online behaviour.

YouTube has become the second most popular search engine globally, with over 2 billion monthly active users. This presents a significant opportunity for businesses to reach their target audience through YouTube advertising.

YouTube's search capabilities also make it an attractive platform for businesses to consider when developing their SEM strategies. With its vast reach and engagement, businesses can leverage YouTube to increase brand awareness, drive traffic to their website, and generate leads.

YouTube's AI-powered targeting capabilities allow businesses to optimise their ad targeting by reaching the most relevant audience for their campaigns. By analysing user demographics, interests, and online behaviour, YouTube's AI can help businesses ensure that their ads are seen by the right audience. YouTube's AI-powered video recommendations algorithm also helps businesses improve their reach by suggesting videos to users based on their viewing history and engagement patterns. Additionally, businesses can leverage YouTube's AI-powered bidding strategies to optimise their ad spend by automatically adjusting bids based on the likelihood of conversions.

AI-powered tools can also help businesses with video content creation and analysis on YouTube. YouTube's Creator Studio offers several AI-powered tools that allow businesses to optimise their video content for maximum engagement. These tools include automated captioning, which generates captions for videos automatically, making them more accessible to viewers. Additionally, YouTube's AI-powered video analytics provides insights into video performance, such as audience retention, engagement, and demographics. This information can help businesses refine their video content and improve their SEM strategies.

With over 300 million active users, Amazon is one of the world's largest online marketplaces, making it a valuable platform for businesses to consider when developing their SEM strategies. Amazon's AI-powered product search capabilities allow businesses to target their audience more effectively by showing their products to users based on their search queries. Additionally, Amazon's AI-powered recommendations engine suggests products to users based on their browsing and purchase history, improving the overall shopping experience. As Amazon continues to grow, its influence in the search and e-commerce industries is only going to increase, making it essential for businesses to understand how to optimise their advertising strategies on the platform.

Amazon's AI-powered ad campaign management tools allow businesses to optimise their advertising strategies and reach their target audience more effectively. Amazon's AI-powered product targeting capabilities enable businesses to show their products to users based on their search queries, increasing the chances of conversions. Additionally, Amazon's AI-powered bidding strategies allow businesses to optimise their ad spend by automatically adjusting bids based on the likelihood of conversions.

To improve product visibility and sales on Amazon, businesses can leverage AI-driven strategies to optimise their advertising campaigns. One strategy is to use Amazon's AI-powered product targeting capabilities to ensure that ads are shown to the most relevant audience. This can be achieved by analysing user search queries and purchase history to ensure that ads are targeted to users who are most likely to convert.

Another strategy is to use Amazon's AI-powered recommendations engine to suggest relevant products to users based on their browsing and purchase history. This can improve the overall shopping experience and increase the chances of conversions. Additionally, businesses can use Amazon's AI-powered bidding strategies to optimise their ad spend by automatically adjusting bids based on the likelihood of conversions.

Social media platforms have become an integral part of modern life, significantly impacting search behaviour and marketing strategies. With over 4.5 billion active users worldwide, social media platforms provide a valuable opportunity for businesses to reach their target audience. Social media's impact on search behaviour has also led to changes in marketing strategies, with businesses now incorporating social media into their SEM strategies. Understanding the impact of social media platforms on search behaviour and marketing is critical for businesses looking to optimise their SEM strategies.

Social media platforms like Facebook, Instagram, Twitter, and LinkedIn are leveraging AI to enhance their ad targeting and optimisation capabilities, providing businesses with new opportunities to reach their target audience more effectively. Social media platforms' AI algorithms analyse user data, such as demographics, interests, and online behaviour, to ensure that ads are shown to the most relevant audience.

Additionally, social media platforms offer AI-powered bidding strategies that optimise ad spending by automatically adjusting bids based on the likelihood of conversions. Businesses can also leverage AI-powered ad creation tools that use machine learning algorithms to optimise ad elements such as images, text, and calls-to-action to improve their effectiveness.

AI can also help businesses with social listening, sentiment analysis, and content curation on social media platforms. Social listening tools powered by AI can monitor social media conversations related to a brand, product, or service and provide insights into audience sentiment, preferences, and behaviour. Sentiment analysis algorithms can also help businesses gauge audience sentiment towards their brand, product, or service, allowing them to refine their marketing strategies. AI-powered content curation tools can also help businesses identify relevant and engaging content to share with their audience, improving their social media presence and driving engagement.

While Google Assistant dominates the voice search market, other virtual assistants like Siri, Alexa, and Cortana also have a significant presence in the industry. These virtual assistants employ AI algorithms to enhance their voice search capabilities, making them essential for businesses to consider when developing their SEM strategies. Understanding the role of voice search in non-Google virtual assistants is critical for businesses looking to reach their target audience effectively.

To optimise their content and ads for voice search on alternative platforms, businesses need to understand how users interact with these virtual assistants. One strategy is to focus on long-tail keywords and natural language queries that users are more likely to use when conducting voice searches. Another strategy is to provide structured data markup for their content, allowing virtual assistants to better understand and display their content in search results. Additionally, businesses can leverage local SEO strategies to improve their visibility in voice searches related to location-based queries.

As the use of virtual assistants and voice search continues to grow, it is becoming increasingly important for businesses to consider their implications for SEM beyond Google. The rise of non-Google virtual assistants like Siri, Alexa, and Cortana is changing the way users interact with search engines and how businesses need to optimise their content and ads to reach their target audience effectively. Voice search is becoming more conversational, natural, and context-specific, requiring businesses to adjust their SEM strategies to stay relevant. As virtual assistants continue to improve their AI capabilities, businesses need to adapt to these changes to stay ahead of the curve.

While Google dominates the search engine industry, niche and industry-specific search engines are becoming increasingly important for businesses operating in specialised markets. These search engines provide users with highly targeted and relevant results, making them valuable for businesses looking to reach their target audience effectively. Understanding the importance of niche and industry-specific search engines is critical for businesses looking to optimise their SEM strategies.

AI can help businesses optimise their content and ads for vertical search engines like Yelp, TripAdvisor, and Indeed. By analysing user data, such as search queries, browsing history, and location, AI algorithms can provide insights into user behaviour, preferences, and intent. This information can help businesses create more targeted and relevant content and ads that are more likely to reach their intended audience. Additionally, businesses can use AI-powered bidding strategies to optimise their ad spend and improve their return on investment (ROI).

As new vertical search engines emerge, businesses can leverage AI to identify new opportunities and optimise their advertising strategies. AI algorithms can help businesses analyse user data to identify emerging trends, behaviours, and preferences, providing valuable insights into new markets and opportunities. Additionally, AI-powered tools can help businesses automate their SEM campaigns, freeing up time and resources to focus on other critical areas of their business. By keeping up with emerging vertical search markets and leveraging AI, businesses can stay ahead of the competition and achieve better results through SEM. Tracking and analysing performance data from various search engines and platforms is essential for businesses looking to measure the success of their SEM campaigns. With so many search engines and platforms available, it can be challenging for businesses to keep track of their advertising performance across different channels. However, it is critical to understand how different platforms perform and how they contribute to the overall success of a business's advertising strategy.

AI-generated insights and recommendations can help businesses adapt their SEM strategies and improve their advertising performance across various search engines and platforms. By analysing performance data, AI algorithms can identify patterns, trends, and opportunities that may not be visible to humans. AI-powered tools can also help businesses automate their SEM campaigns, making it easier to adjust their strategies based on real time performance data.

Balancing investments in Google and alternative search platforms is critical for businesses looking to optimise their SEM campaigns. While Google dominates the search engine industry, other platforms like Bing, Amazon, and social media platforms also offer valuable opportunities for businesses to reach their target audience. However, allocating resources across different search platforms requires careful consideration of business goals, target audience, and available resources.

To prepare for the future of AI and SEM beyond Google, it is essential for businesses to stay informed about emerging search engines, platforms, and technologies. As AI continues to advance, new opportunities for businesses to optimise their SEM strategies will emerge. Keeping up with these developments requires a willingness to learn and adapt, as well as a commitment to staying informed about industry trends and developments.

As the search landscape continues to evolve, businesses must adapt their SEM strategies to stay relevant and competitive. This requires a focus on AI-driven opportunities, such as leveraging AI to optimise ad targeting, bidding strategies, and content creation. Additionally, businesses need to be willing to experiment with new platforms and technologies as they emerge, such as voice search and emerging search engines. By embracing new technologies and approaches and being open to change, businesses can stay ahead of the curve and achieve better results through SEM.

To prepare for the future of AI and SEM beyond Google, businesses must embrace a multi-platform approach to SEM. This approach involves leveraging multiple search engines and platforms to reach their target audience more effectively, rather than relying solely on Google. By diversifying their SEM strategies, businesses can improve their visibility, reach new audiences, and reduce their reliance on any single platform. Additionally, a multi-platform approach to SEM can help businesses stay competitive as new search engines and platforms emerge.

Harnessing the power of AI and SEM across multiple platforms is essential for businesses looking to achieve their advertising goals and prepare for the future of SEM beyond Google. As AI continues to advance, new opportunities for businesses to optimise their SEM strategies will emerge, and a multi-platform approach to SEM will become increasingly important. By leveraging AI to improve ad targeting, bidding strategies, and content creation, businesses can improve their advertising performance across various search engines and platforms. Additionally, businesses can stay ahead of the curve by staying informed about emerging search engines, platforms, and technologies and adapting to the evolving search landscape.

Diversifying your search engine marketing strategy beyond Google can bring many benefits to businesses. By leveraging multiple search engines and platforms, businesses can reach a broader audience and improve their visibility, reducing their reliance on any single platform. Additionally, alternative search engines and platforms may offer lower competition and lower cost per click, providing cost-effective opportunities for businesses to reach their target audience. Diversifying your SEM strategy beyond Google also allows businesses to stay ahead of the curve by adapting to the evolving search landscape and embracing new technologies and approaches.

Embracing AI is becoming increasingly important for businesses looking to succeed in the competitive digital landscape. With so much data available, it can be challenging for businesses to analyse and make sense of it all without the help of AI. AI can provide valuable insights into audience behaviour, preferences, and intent, allowing businesses to create more targeted and effective advertising campaigns. Additionally, AI-powered tools can help businesses automate their SEM campaigns, saving time and resources and improving advertising performance. In this chapter, we have explored how businesses can leverage AI to optimise their SEM strategies across various search engines and platforms, providing valuable insights and strategies for embracing AI to drive success in the competitive digital landscape.

Chapter Eight: AI and Social Media Marketing

Social media marketing has become an integral part of digital marketing strategies in recent years, and the role of AI in enhancing social media marketing efforts cannot be overlooked. With the vast amounts of data generated by social media platforms, AI-powered tools and algorithms can provide valuable insights into user behaviour, preferences, and intent, enabling businesses to create more targeted and effective social media campaigns.

Social media has become an increasingly important component of digital marketing strategies in recent years. With billions of users across various social media platforms, businesses can reach a vast audience and build brand awareness and engagement in ways that were not possible before. Social media platforms offer businesses the opportunity to interact with customers directly, providing valuable insights into customer preferences and behaviour. As social media continues to grow in popularity, businesses must continue to evolve their social media marketing strategies to stay competitive.

AI is transforming the way businesses approach social media marketing by providing insights and tools that were previously unavailable. With the vast amounts of data generated by social media platforms, AI-powered tools and algorithms can analyse user behaviour, preferences, and intent, enabling businesses to create more targeted and effective social media campaigns. Additionally, AI can automate various aspects of social media marketing, freeing up time and resources for businesses to focus on other critical areas of their business. By leveraging AI, businesses can gain a competitive advantage in the rapidly evolving world of social media marketing.

AI-driven content creation and curation have become increasingly popular in social media marketing. With the vast amounts of data generated by social media platforms, businesses can use AI-powered tools to create and curate content that resonates with their target audience. AI algorithms can analyse user behaviour, preferences, and intent, identifying patterns and trends that can inform content creation and curation strategies. AI can automate content creation and curation processes, saving time and resources for businesses.

AI tools can be used to generate compelling and engaging social media content, helping businesses save time and resources while still creating content that resonates with their target audience. AI algorithms can analyse user behaviour, preferences, and intent, identifying patterns and trends that can inform content creation strategies. Additionally, AI can generate content in various formats, such as images, videos, and text, tailored to the specific needs and preferences of the target audience. By leveraging AI for content creation, businesses can improve their social media marketing efforts, creating engaging and relevant content that drives engagement and brand awareness.

AI can also be leveraged for content curation and personalisation on social media platforms. With the vast amounts of content available on social media platforms, it can be challenging for businesses to curate and share content that is relevant and engaging to their target audience. AI algorithms can analyse user behaviour, preferences, and intent, identifying patterns and trends that can inform content curation strategies. AI can also personalise content recommendations and delivery based on individual user behaviour and preferences, creating a more personalised and engaging social media experience for users. By leveraging AI for content curation and personalisation, businesses can improve their social media marketing efforts, driving engagement and brand awareness.

AI-powered audience targeting and segmentation can help businesses reach the right audience with the right message at the right time. With the vast amounts of data generated by social media platforms, AI algorithms can analyse user behaviour, preferences, and intent, identifying patterns and trends that can inform audience targeting and segmentation strategies. Additionally, AI can automate various aspects of audience targeting and segmentation, saving time and resources for businesses. By leveraging AI for audience targeting and segmentation, businesses can improve their social media marketing efforts, driving engagement and conversions.

AI plays a critical role in audience identification and targeting on social media platforms. With the vast amounts of data generated by social media platforms, AI-powered algorithms can analyse user behaviour, preferences, and intent, identifying patterns and trends that can inform audience identification and targeting strategies. Additionally, AI can segment audiences based on various demographic, behavioural, and psychographic factors, creating more targeted and effective social media campaigns. By leveraging AI for audience identification and targeting, businesses can improve their social media marketing efforts, driving engagement and conversions.

Implementing AI-driven techniques for creating precise audience segments can help businesses reach the right audience with the right message at the right time. AI algorithms can analyse vast amounts of data generated by social media platforms, including demographic, behavioural, and psychographic data, to create precise audience segments. AI-powered tools can automate the audience segmentation process, saving time and resources for businesses while creating more targeted and effective social media campaigns. By leveraging AI for audience segmentation, businesses can improve their social media marketing efforts, driving engagement and conversions.

AI and social media advertising have become increasingly intertwined in recent years. With the vast amounts of data generated by social media platforms, AI-powered algorithms can analyse user behaviour, preferences, and intent, enabling businesses to create more targeted and effective social media ad campaigns. Additionally, AI can automate various aspects of social media advertising, such as ad creation, placement, and optimisation, saving time and resources for businesses while improving advertising performance.

Social media ad platforms, such as Facebook, Instagram, Twitter, and LinkedIn, have all incorporated AI capabilities into their advertising tools. AI algorithms can analyse vast amounts of user data to identify patterns and trends that can inform ad targeting, ad creation, and ad optimisation strategies. Additionally, AI can automate various aspects of social media advertising, such as ad placement and bidding, saving time and resources for businesses while improving advertising performance.

AI can be used to optimise ad targeting, bidding, and budget allocation on social media platforms. With the vast amounts of user data generated by social media platforms, AI algorithms can analyse user behaviour, preferences, and intent, identifying patterns and trends that can inform ad targeting and bidding strategies. Additionally, AI can automate the ad bidding process, adjusting bids in real time to optimise ad performance while staying within the allocated budget. By leveraging AI for ad targeting, bidding, and budget allocation, businesses can improve their social media advertising performance, driving engagement and conversions.

AI-driven tools for ad creative testing and performance analysis can help businesses identify and optimise their most effective social media ads. AI algorithms can analyse vast amounts of ad performance data, identifying patterns and trends that can inform ad creative testing and optimisation strategies. Additionally, AI-powered tools can automate the ad creative testing and performance analysis process, saving time and resources for businesses while providing more accurate and detailed insights into ad performance. By leveraging AI-driven tools for ad creative testing and performance analysis, businesses can improve their social media advertising efforts, creating more effective ads that drive engagement and conversions.

AI and social listening have become increasingly important in social media marketing. Social listening involves monitoring and analysing social media conversations around specific keywords, topics, or brands. AI-powered algorithms can analyse vast amounts of social media data, identifying patterns and trends that can inform social media marketing strategies. Additionally, AI can automate various aspects of social listening, such as data collection and analysis, saving time and resources for businesses while providing more accurate and detailed insights into customer behaviour and preferences.

AI can be leveraged for monitoring social media conversations and trends, allowing businesses to gain valuable insights into customer behaviour and preferences. With the vast amounts of social media data generated daily, it can be challenging for businesses to monitor and analyse all relevant conversations and trends manually. AI-powered algorithms can analyse social media data, including text, images, and videos, identifying patterns and trends that can inform social media marketing strategies. Additionally, AI can automate data collection and analysis, saving time and resources for businesses while providing more accurate and detailed insights. By leveraging AI for monitoring social media conversations and trends, businesses can improve their social media marketing efforts, driving engagement and conversions.

Utilising AI-powered sentiment analysis is another way businesses can leverage AI in social media marketing. Sentiment analysis involves analysing social media conversations to determine the overall sentiment or opinion around a particular topic, brand, or product. AI algorithms can analyse text data to identify sentiment, whether positive, negative, or neutral, providing valuable insights into customer opinions and feedback. By leveraging AI for sentiment analysis, businesses can gain a better understanding of how customers perceive their brand, products, or services and adjust their social media marketing strategies accordingly. This can help businesses improve their social media presence, increase engagement and conversions, and build stronger relationships with their customers.

Implementing AI-driven insights is crucial for businesses to inform their social media marketing strategies and improve the overall customer experience. AI algorithms can analyse social media data, identifying patterns and trends that can inform marketing strategies, such as content creation, audience targeting, and ad optimisation. Additionally, AI can automate various aspects of social media marketing, such as content scheduling and engagement tracking, saving time and resources for businesses while improving customer experience. By leveraging AI-driven insights, businesses can create more targeted and effective social media marketing strategies, driving engagement and conversions while providing a better customer experience.

AI and influencer marketing are becoming increasingly intertwined as businesses seek more effective ways to reach their target audiences. Influencer marketing involves partnering with individuals who have a strong following on social media to promote products or services. AI-powered algorithms can analyse social media data, identifying potential influencers based on their audience demographics, engagement rates, and other factors. Additionally, AI can help businesses measure the effectiveness of their influencer marketing campaigns, tracking metrics such as reach, engagement, and conversions. By leveraging AI in influencer marketing, businesses can identify the most effective influencers for their campaigns and measure their performance accurately.

AI can play a crucial role in identifying and assessing potential influencers for collaboration. With the vast number of influencers available on social media, it can be challenging for businesses to manually identify the most relevant and effective ones for their campaigns. AI algorithms can analyse social media data, including follower count, engagement rates, and audience demographics, to identify potential influencers who align with a business's target audience and goals. Additionally, AI can help businesses assess the authenticity and influence of potential influencers, ensuring that they are a good fit for their brand and campaign objectives. By leveraging AI for influencer identification and assessment, businesses can improve the effectiveness of their influencer marketing campaigns and reach a larger, more engaged audience.

AI-driven tools can be used to track influencer performance and calculate the return on investment (ROI) of influencer marketing campaigns. AI algorithms can analyse social media data, tracking metrics such as reach, engagement, and conversions to measure the effectiveness of influencer collaborations. AI can automate the process of collecting and analysing influencer performance data, providing accurate and detailed insights into campaign performance. By leveraging AI-driven tools for influencer performance tracking and ROI calculation, businesses can measure the success of their influencer marketing efforts and make data-driven decisions to improve future campaigns.

Leveraging AI insights is essential for businesses to optimise their influencer marketing strategies continually. AI algorithms can analyse social media data, identifying patterns and trends that can inform influencer marketing strategies, such as influencer selection, content creation, and campaign optimisation. AI can help businesses track the performance of their influencer marketing campaigns in real time, providing insights into what is working and what needs improvement. By leveraging AI insights, businesses can adjust their influencer marketing strategies and improve the effectiveness of their campaigns. This can lead to increased engagement and conversions, strengthening the relationship between the brand and its audience.

Social media analytics is a crucial component of social media marketing, providing insights into audience behaviour, campaign performance, and other valuable metrics. AI is transforming the way businesses approach social media analytics, automating data collection and analysis while providing deeper insights into audience behaviour and campaign performance. AI algorithms can analyse social media data in real time, identifying patterns and trends that can inform marketing strategies and drive business growth. Additionally, AI can help businesses measure the effectiveness of their social media marketing campaigns accurately, tracking metrics such as reach, engagement, and conversions. By leveraging AI in social media analytics, businesses can gain a better understanding of their audience and adjust their social media marketing strategies to improve performance continually.

AI-powered analytics tools are becoming increasingly popular for businesses to track their social media performance. AI algorithms can analyse social media data in real time tracking metrics such as follower growth, engagement rates, and content performance. By leveraging AI-powered analytics tools, businesses can gain a better understanding of their audience's behaviour and preferences, adjust their content strategies accordingly, and increase engagement and conversions. AI can automate the process of collecting and analysing social media data, providing businesses with accurate and timely insights into their social media performance.

One of the most significant benefits of AI-powered social media analytics is the ability to extract actionable insights from social media data. AI algorithms can analyse social media data, identifying patterns and trends that can inform marketing strategies and drive business growth. By leveraging AI-generated insights, businesses can adjust their social media marketing strategies and improve the effectiveness of their campaigns. For example, AI can help businesses identify which types of content are most effective at driving engagement and conversions, enabling them to focus on creating more of this content. Additionally, AI can help businesses identify the most effective social media platforms for reaching their target audience, informing advertising and content strategies.

Adapting social media strategies based on AI-driven recommendations is a critical component of AI-powered social media marketing. AI algorithms can analyse social media data, identifying patterns and trends that can inform marketing strategies and drive business growth. By leveraging AI-driven recommendations, businesses can adjust their social media marketing strategies and improve the effectiveness of their campaigns. For example, AI can suggest the optimal posting times and frequency for a business's social media content based on audience behaviour and engagement patterns. By adopting social media strategies based on AI-driven recommendations, businesses can maximise the impact of their social media marketing efforts and drive business growth.

Social media automation is the process of using software tools to automate social media marketing tasks, such as scheduling posts and engaging with followers. AI is transforming the way businesses approach social media automation, providing advanced tools and technologies that can automate complex tasks and improve efficiency. For example, AI-powered chatbots can interact with customers on social media platforms, providing personalised recommendations and answering frequently asked questions. AI can automate the process of content creation, generating social media posts based on a business's specific audience and marketing objectives. By leveraging AI in social media automation, businesses can streamline their social media marketing processes, save time and resources, and improve engagement and conversions.

AI-driven chatbots and virtual assistants are transforming the way businesses approach customer support and engagement on social media platforms. AI-powered chatbots can interact with customers on social media platforms, providing personalised recommendations and answering frequently asked questions. These chatbots use natural language processing and machine learning algorithms to understand the customer's intent and provide relevant responses, improving the customer experience and reducing the workload on customer support teams. Additionally, AI-powered virtual assistants can engage with customers on social media platforms, providing personalised product recommendations and offers. By implementing AI-driven chatbots and virtual assistants for customer support and engagement, businesses can save time and resources, improve customer satisfaction, and increase conversions.

AI-powered tools for social media scheduling, posting, and monitoring are transforming the way businesses approach social media marketing. AI algorithms can analyse social media data, identify the optimal times and frequency for posting content, and automatically schedule posts accordingly. Additionally, AI-powered tools can analyse social media data in real time, tracking metrics such as follower growth, engagement rates, and content performance. By leveraging AI-powered tools for social media scheduling, posting, and monitoring, businesses can save time and resources, increase the efficiency of their social media marketing efforts, and improve engagement and conversions. Furthermore, AI can help businesses monitor social media conversations and trends, identify potential issues and opportunities, and adjust their social media strategies accordingly.

Balancing automation and human interaction is a critical consideration for businesses looking to leverage AI in their social media marketing efforts. While AI-powered tools and technologies can improve efficiency and effectiveness, it's essential to maintain a balance between automation and human interaction to ensure a positive customer experience. For example, businesses should use AI-powered chatbots and virtual assistants to handle simple customer inquiries and routine tasks but ensure that there is a way for customers to speak with a human representative if necessary. However, businesses should avoid relying solely on AI-powered tools for social media content creation and curation, ensuring that there is a human touch in their content strategy to maintain authenticity and connection with their audience. By striking a balance between automation and human interaction, businesses can maximise the benefits of AI-powered social media marketing while still providing a personalised and authentic customer experience.

As AI continues to transform the way businesses approach social media marketing, it's essential to prepare for the future of AI and social media marketing. AI-powered tools and technologies are constantly evolving, and businesses must stay up-to-date with the latest developments to remain competitive in the digital landscape. Additionally, as AI becomes more integrated into social media marketing, it's essential to understand the potential risks and ethical considerations associated with AI-powered social media marketing.

Staying informed about emerging AI technologies is crucial for businesses looking to leverage AI in their social media marketing efforts. As AI continues to evolve, new tools and technologies are emerging that can help businesses improve the efficiency and effectiveness of their social media marketing strategies. By staying up-to-date with the latest developments in AI, businesses can identify new opportunities for innovation and stay ahead of the competition. Understanding the potential impact of emerging AI technologies on social media marketing is crucial for businesses to stay ahead of the curve and prepare for future changes in the digital landscape.

Adapting to changes in social media algorithms and user behaviour is crucial for businesses looking to leverage AI in their social media marketing efforts. Social media algorithms are constantly evolving, and businesses must stay up-to-date with the latest changes to ensure that their content remains visible and engaging to their target audience. Additionally, as user behaviour on social media platforms changes, businesses must adapt their social media marketing strategies to ensure that they are reaching their target audience effectively. By leveraging AI-powered tools and technologies to analyse social media data and identify changes in algorithms and user behaviour, businesses can adapt their social media marketing strategies in real time, improving their efficiency and effectiveness.

Integrating AI into long-term social media marketing strategies is crucial for businesses looking to remain competitive in the digital landscape. As AI continues to transform the way businesses approach social media marketing, integrating AI-powered tools and technologies into long-term social media marketing strategies can help businesses improve their efficiency and effectiveness, reach new audiences, and drive business growth. By leveraging AI-powered tools and technologies for content creation, audience targeting, advertising, social listening, and automation, businesses can enhance their social media marketing efforts and achieve long-term success.

By leveraging AI-powered tools and technologies for content creation, audience targeting, advertising, social listening, and automation, businesses can enhance their social media marketing efforts and achieve long-term success. However, it's important to approach AI-powered social media marketing with an ethical and responsible mindset, considering the potential risks and ethical considerations associated with AI. Additionally, staying informed about emerging AI technologies and adapting to changes in social media algorithms and user behaviour is crucial for businesses to remain competitive in the digital landscape. By embracing AI for social media marketing success, businesses can reach new audiences, drive business growth, and achieve long-term success in the digital age.

Incorporating AI into social media marketing efforts has numerous benefits for businesses. AI-powered tools and technologies can help businesses improve the efficiency and effectiveness of their social media marketing strategies by automating tedious tasks, identifying new opportunities for innovation, and providing valuable insights into audience behaviour and preferences. AI can help businesses create more compelling and engaging social media content, personalise their marketing efforts to reach specific audience segments and optimise their social media advertising campaigns for maximum ROI.

By leveraging AI-powered social listening tools, businesses can gain valuable insights into customer opinions and feedback, enabling them to improve their products and services and provide a better customer experience. Ultimately, incorporating AI into social media marketing efforts can help businesses achieve long-term success and drive business growth in the digital age.

Staying ahead of the curve in an increasingly AI-driven marketing landscape is crucial for businesses looking to remain competitive and achieve long-term success. As AI continues to transform the way businesses approach social media marketing, it's important for businesses to stay informed about emerging AI technologies and trends and to adapt their social media marketing strategies accordingly. By staying ahead of the curve and embracing AI-powered tools and technologies for social media marketing, businesses can gain a competitive edge, reach new audiences, and drive business growth. Additionally, businesses must approach AI-powered social media marketing with an ethical and responsible mindset, considering the potential risks and ethical considerations associated with AI.

Fostering a culture of innovation and adaptability is essential for businesses looking to excel in social media marketing. As AI continues to transform the way businesses approach social media marketing, it's crucial for businesses to embrace a mindset of continuous improvement and innovation and to be adaptable to changing market trends and consumer preferences. By fostering a culture of innovation and adaptability, businesses can encourage their teams to experiment with new ideas, technologies, and approaches to social media marketing and to constantly seek out new opportunities for improvement and growth. By promoting a culture of innovation and adaptability, businesses can create an environment that values creativity, collaboration, and risk-taking, fostering a more dynamic and agile approach to social media marketing.

Chapter Nine: AI and Multilingual SEO

With the rise of Google search and other search engines, businesses of all sizes can access a global market. This has increased the need for effective multilingual SEO strategies that cater to audiences in different languages and regions. The implementation of AI in multilingual SEO has the potential to transform how businesses approach global marketing. AI technologies can help companies to identify relevant keywords, translate content accurately, and improve website accessibility for multilingual audiences.

As businesses expand their reach beyond their home markets, the need to target international audiences through SEO grows in importance. The ability to reach potential customers in different languages and regions is crucial for success in today's global economy. AI plays an increasingly significant role in multilingual SEO, offering new opportunities for businesses to expand their reach and connect with diverse audiences worldwide.

With the help of AI, companies can improve their ability to target and reach audiences in different languages and regions. AI-powered tools can help businesses to identify the right keywords, create content that resonates with target audiences, and adapt to changes in local search algorithms. This chapter will explore how AI is transforming multilingual SEO strategies and helping businesses to achieve success in global markets.

AI-powered language detection tools can analyse the language of the website content, allowing businesses to understand the languages used by their target audience.

These tools can help identify the languages that are most commonly used in specific geographic areas, which is crucial for multilingual SEO strategies. By using AI to detect languages, businesses can create and optimise their website content in the languages that their target audience speaks. AI language detection tools can also help identify and eliminate duplicate content across different language versions of a website, which can negatively impact SEO performance.

AI-powered language detection can also be used to optimise multilingual SEO strategies by ensuring that content is accurately labelled with the correct language and that search engines can crawl and index it effectively. This is particularly important for websites that target multiple countries or regions with different languages. AI algorithms can analyse a piece's structure, syntax, and vocabulary to determine the language used, allowing businesses to optimise their content for the specific languages they are targeting.

These tools use machine learning algorithms to automatically detect the language of a website, webpage, or content. This information is then used to provide targeted search results to users who search in a particular language. By identifying the language of a webpage, search engines can serve more relevant results to users, improving the user experience and increasing the chances of the webpage being ranked higher in search results.

When it comes to multilingual SEO, identifying and targeting high-potential keywords for different languages and regions is crucial for success. AI can play a significant role in this process by helping businesses conduct multilingual keyword analysis and selection. AI can analyse data from various sources and provide insights into relevant keywords and phrases in different languages. This enables businesses to identify the right keywords to target in their multilingual SEO strategy, which can help improve their search engine rankings in other regions and countries. They can assist in identifying the most relevant and high-traffic keywords in different languages and regions, taking into account cultural nuances, local trends, and search volume. AI-powered tools can help identify regional language variations and synonyms of targeted keywords, ensuring that the content is optimised for the specific region or country. Companies can increase their visibility and reach international audiences by targeting high-potential keywords in different languages and regions.

AI has transformed the way businesses approach content translation for multilingual SEO. With AI-powered tools, it is now possible to translate content efficiently and accurately while retaining the original meaning and tone. These tools use advanced algorithms and natural language processing (NLP) techniques to analyse the source content and generate high-quality translations in different languages. Additionally, AI-powered translation tools can learn from user feedback and continuously improve their performance over time, making them valuable assets for businesses targeting international markets.

AI-driven translation technologies are computer programs that use machine learning algorithms to translate text from one language to another automatically. These tools use large datasets of parallel texts to learn how to recognise patterns in language and how to solve them accurately. Some popular AI-driven translation tools include Google Translate, Microsoft Translator, and Amazon Translate.

AI-powered translation tools can be beneficial for creating multilingual content for SEO. These tools use machine learning algorithms to translate content automatically from one language to another, and they continue to improve as they receive more input data. These tools can save time and resources compared to manual translation. They can also help ensure accuracy and consistency across different languages. However, it is essential to note that machine translation is not always perfect and may require human review and editing to ensure the highest quality of the translated content.

While AI-powered translation tools have become increasingly sophisticated, there is still a need for human review to ensure accuracy and cultural sensitivity. It's essential to strike the right balance between using AI-generated translations for efficiency and cost-effectiveness and having human reviewers check for errors and cultural nuances. AI tools can help speed up the translation process and reduce costs, but they should only be relied on with human oversight. Ultimately, the goal is to create high-quality, engaging content that resonates with multilingual audiences. A combination of AI and human translation can help achieve this.

AI can play a critical role in cultural adaptation in multilingual SEO. Cultural adaptation is modifying a website's content and messaging to fit the target audience's local customs, beliefs, and behaviours. AI-powered tools can help identify these cultural nuances, providing insights into how to tailor content for specific regions or audiences. This includes considerations such as local slang, customs, and holidays. By leveraging AI for cultural adaptation, businesses can create a more personalised experience for their international audience, leading to better engagement and conversion rates.

One of multilingual SEO's main challenges is ensuring that the content created for different regions is culturally adapted. AI can help with this by analysing and understanding cultural nuances and adjusting the content accordingly. For example, an AI tool can identify idiomatic expressions and colloquialisms that might not make sense in a different cultural context and suggest alternative phrasings that are more appropriate. By leveraging AI in this way, businesses can ensure that their content is translated accurately, culturally relevant, and suitable for their target audience.

Regarding international link building, AI can help identify and assess potential multilingual backlink opportunities. Companies can use AI-powered tools to analyse websites and identify pages with high domain authority, relevant content, and potential link-building opportunities. Automating the link-building process and ensuring that link-building efforts focus on the most promising opportunities can save time and effort. AI can also be used to analyse link-building campaigns and provide insights on which strategies are most effective in generating backlinks in different language regions.

AI-powered tools can be leveraged for streamlining and optimising international link-building campaigns. AI can help identify potential international backlink opportunities by providing insights on the most relevant and authoritative websites for a particular language and region. By analysing user behaviour and language preferences, AI can also offer insights into the type of content that would be most engaging for a particular target audience, allowing businesses to create more effective link-building strategies. Additionally, AI can help monitor the performance of international backlinks and provide recommendations for optimising them to improve search engine rankings.

AI can extract insights from the large amount of data generated by multilingual SEO campaigns. AI-powered analytics tools can help track the performance of multilingual SEO campaigns across different languages and regions, providing valuable insights into which strategies are working and which are not. These tools can also help identify patterns and trends in user behaviour across different markets, which can inform future multilingual SEO strategies. Additionally, AI can be used to perform competitive analysis across other markets, identifying which companies are ranking well for specific keywords and identifying opportunities for improvement.

Multilingual SEO analytics is crucial in identifying the success of your strategies. AI-powered analytics tools can track performance metrics across multiple languages and regions. These tools can help you understand how different regions interact with your content, identify patterns and opportunities for improvement, and generate actionable insights for your SEO strategy. With AI, you can leverage predictive analytics to predict future trends and outcomes and optimise your SEO campaigns accordingly.

With the help of AI-driven analytics, businesses can monitor and evaluate the performance of their multilingual SEO strategies. They can use AI-powered tools to extract actionable insights and identify areas for improvement. Based on these insights, businesses can adapt their multilingual SEO strategies to achieve better results and optimise their content for different languages and regions. For instance, AI can help enterprises to identify which languages or regions are driving the most traffic or conversions, which keywords are performing well, and which content is resonating with users in different languages. These insights can inform future multilingual SEO strategies and help businesses stay ahead of the competition.

AI can also help businesses extract actionable insights from multilingual SEO data. By using machine learning algorithms, AI tools can analyse vast amounts of data from multiple sources to identify patterns, trends, and opportunities for optimisation. AI can also provide real time performance metrics for different languages and regions, allowing businesses to make data-driven decisions and adjust their strategies accordingly. Furthermore, AI can help identify the most effective multilingual SEO tactics and recommend changes to improve campaign performance over time. By harnessing the power of AI analytics, businesses can gain a competitive advantage in the global marketplace and drive more traffic, leads, and conversions from their multilingual SEO efforts.

The rise of voice search in international markets has been rapid, with a significant increase in voice-activated devices and smart speakers being used worldwide. As a result, businesses that target global markets need to consider how to optimise their multilingual SEO strategies for voice search. This is where AI comes into play, providing tools and techniques for multilingual voice search optimization to help businesses improve their visibility and reach in global markets.

As voice search continues to gain popularity in international markets, it's important to adopt multilingual SEO strategies to optimise this type of search using AI technologies. This includes understanding the nuances of different languages and accents and optimising for long-tail and conversational queries. AI-powered tools can help with voice search optimisation by providing insights into the most common voice search queries and identifying opportunities for natural language processing and optimisation. Additionally, using structured data markup can help search engines better understand and interpret the content, improving its chances of appearing in voice search results.

As AI technology advances, businesses must stay informed about emerging AI technologies and their potential impact on multilingual SEO. This includes staying up-to-date on new language detection techniques, translation technologies, and cultural adaptation tools. Additionally, it is crucial to adapt to changes in search engine algorithms and user behaviour, particularly as voice search becomes increasingly popular in international markets. Integrating AI into long-term multilingual SEO strategies can help businesses stay ahead of the curve and succeed in global markets.

As with any aspect of SEO, it is essential to stay informed about emerging technologies and their potential impact on the field. This includes staying up to date with advancements in AI that may affect multilingual SEO. Keeping an eye on developments in machine learning, natural language processing, and other related fields can help businesses stay ahead of the curve and adapt their strategies accordingly. Additionally, monitoring changes in search engine algorithms and user behaviour in different regions and languages can provide valuable insights into where multilingual SEO is headed.

As with any SEO strategy, it is vital to stay up to date with changes in search engine algorithms and global user behaviour. This includes understanding how AI is being integrated into search engines and how it affects search results. It is also essential to monitor how user behaviour changes, particularly regarding voice search and the increasing use of mobile devices. By staying informed and adapting strategies accordingly, businesses can continue to succeed in the global market.

As AI continues to evolve and impact multilingual SEO, it's important to integrate AI-driven tools and techniques into long-term strategies. This means continuously staying up-to-date with emerging technologies and trends in the industry, as well as regular monitoring and adapting to changes in search engine algorithms and user behaviour. Also, fostering a culture of innovation and adaptability can help businesses stay ahead of the curve and succeed in global markets.

The benefits of incorporating AI into multilingual SEO efforts are significant. AI can help with language detection, keyword analysis and selection, content translation, cultural adaptation, international link building, and multilingual SEO analytics. By leveraging AI technologies, businesses can improve their multilingual SEO strategies and reach new audiences in global markets. Staying informed about emerging AI technologies and adapting to changes in search engine algorithms and user behaviour is crucial to staying ahead of the curve in an increasingly global and AI-driven marketing landscape. By fostering a culture of innovation and adaptability, businesses can excel in multilingual SEO and achieve long-term success.

Integrating AI into multilingual SEO brings various benefits, such as improved accuracy, efficiency and scalability. AI-powered language detection and translation tools can help identify and target high-potential keywords for different languages and regions and create multilingual content for SEO. AI-powered analytics tools can also track multilingual SEO performance and extract actionable insights for adapting strategies based on AI-driven recommendations. Overall, AI can enhance the effectiveness and impact of multilingual SEO strategies in targeting global markets.

The importance of effective multilingual SEO cannot be overstated as the global market continues to grow and become more interconnected. Incorporating AI into multilingual SEO efforts can provide numerous benefits, including improved accuracy and efficiency in keyword research, content translation, and cultural adaptation. AI-powered tools can also help identify and assess potential international backlink opportunities, track multilingual SEO performance, and extract actionable insights to improve strategies over time. By staying ahead of the curve in an increasingly AI-driven global marketing landscape, businesses can gain a significant competitive advantage and achieve tremendous success in reaching international audiences.

Incorporating AI into multilingual SEO strategies presents a valuable opportunity to reach global markets and expand business growth. Businesses can create effective multilingual SEO strategies that resonate with diverse audiences by leveraging AI-powered tools for language detection, keyword analysis, content translation, and cultural adaptation. However, it is essential to stay informed about emerging AI technologies and adapt to changes in search engine algorithms and user behaviour. Fostering a culture of innovation and adaptability can help businesses stay ahead of the curve and excel in multilingual SEO.

Chapter Ten: AI and Local SEO

Local SEO has become an essential component of any successful digital marketing strategy as the world becomes increasingly digitised. Local SEO helps businesses optimise their online presence to increase visibility in search results for local customers. With the rise of AI, companies can now leverage advanced technologies to achieve even greater success with local SEO. AI-powered tools and technologies can help businesses automate tedious tasks, gain valuable insights into local customer behaviour, and improve the effectiveness of their local SEO strategies.

Local SEO has a significant impact on businesses targeting specific geographic areas. By optimising their online presence for local search, companies can increase their visibility to potential customers actively searching for products or services in their area. Local SEO is particularly important for small and medium-sised businesses, as it enables them to compete with larger, more established companies in their local market. With the right regional SEO strategy in place, businesses can attract more foot traffic, generate more leads, and ultimately drive more sales. By harnessing the power of AI, companies can take their local SEO efforts to the next level, gaining a competitive edge and reaching new audiences.

AI is transforming local SEO strategies in several ways, enabling businesses to achieve even greater success in their local markets. One of the primary ways AI is transforming local SEO is through its ability to automate repetitive tasks, such as keyword research and content optimisation. Businesses can save time and resources by automating these tasks while achieving better results. AI is also making gaining valuable insights into local customer behaviour easier, enabling business owners to better understand their target audience's needs and preferences. This, in turn, allows businesses to tailor their local SEO strategies to meet the needs of their local customers better. Additionally, AI-powered tools can help companies to stay on top of changes in local search algorithms and stay ahead of the competition.

Local keyword research is an essential component of any effective regional SEO strategy. With AI-powered tools and technologies, businesses can take their local keyword research to the next level, gaining deeper insights into the keywords and phrases that their local customers use to search for products and services. AI-powered keyword research tools can help businesses identify high-value keywords that their competitors may be overlooking and uncover long-tail keywords that can help drive more targeted traffic to their websites.

AI-powered tools can play a critical role in local keyword analysis and selection, helping businesses to identify the most relevant and effective keywords for their local SEO campaigns. By leveraging machine learning algorithms, these tools can analyse vast amounts of data to identify patterns and insights that may not be immediately apparent to human analysts. They can also help businesses identify high-intent keywords that are likely to convert into sales or leads, as well as uncover long-tail keywords that competitors may overlook. With these insights, companies can optimise their local keyword selection and improve their local SEO performance, driving more targeted traffic to their website and ultimately achieving tremendous success in their local markets.

Identifying and targeting high-potential local keywords is critical to achieving success with local SEO, and AI can play a significant role in this process. By leveraging machine learning algorithms, businesses can analyse vast amounts of data to identify patterns and insights that can help them identify the keywords with the most significant potential to drive traffic and conversions in their local markets. AI-powered keyword analysis tools can help businesses identify high-intent keywords that are likely to convert and uncover long-tail keywords that competitors may overlook.

AI can also be used to optimise local content, ensuring it is highly relevant and effective for the target audience. Machine learning algorithms can analyse user behaviour and preferences data to identify the types of content most likely to engage and convert local customers. By leveraging this data, businesses can create more targeted and compelling content optimised for local SEO. AI-powered content analysis tools can also help companies to optimise the content structure, tone, and formatting for maximum impact in local markets. With these insights, businesses can create highly effective local content that drives traffic, conversions, and revenue.

AI can also be used to optimise local content, ensuring that it is highly relevant and effective for the target audience. Machine learning algorithms can analyse data on user behaviour and preferences to identify the types of content that are most likely to engage and convert local customers. By leveraging this data, businesses can create more targeted and compelling content optimised for local SEO. AI-powered content analysis tools can also help companies to optimise the content structure, tone, and formatting for maximum impact in local markets. With these insights, businesses can create highly effective local content that drives traffic, conversions, and revenue.

Businesses can leverage AI-powered tools to optimise local website content for better visibility and engagement. With machine learning algorithms, companies can analyse search data and customer behaviour to identify the keywords and phrases that are most relevant to local search queries. AI can also be used to suggest optimised meta titles, descriptions, and header tags, which can help search engines better understand the regional focus of a business. Additionally, AI can assist in optimising website content for local intent by identifying the most commonly searched queries in a local area and incorporating them into the content. By leveraging AI-powered tools for local content optimisation, businesses can increase their visibility in local search results and attract more qualified traffic to their websites.

Incorporating local keywords and context into content is essential for improved local SEO performance, and AI can assist in this process. AI-powered tools can analyse local search data to identify the most relevant local keywords and phrases to incorporate into website content. This process ensures that the content created is tailored to the local area and is optimised for local search queries. Additionally, AI can help businesses incorporate local context into their content, such as local landmarks, events, or news. By doing so, companies can establish themselves as authoritative and relevant within the local community, improving local search rankings and increasing visibility. With the help of AI, businesses can optimise their website content for local search queries and improve their local SEO performance.

Local business listings play a critical role in local SEO, and AI can help businesses optimise their listings for improved visibility and search rankings. AI-powered tools can analyse and update business listings across multiple directories and platforms, ensuring that all information is accurate and consistent. This process can also help businesses identify and rectify any inconsistencies or errors in their listings, which can have a negative impact on local search rankings. Additionally, AI can help businesses identify new directories and platforms to list their business on, further increasing their visibility and reach.

Google My Business is one of the most important local business directories. AI-powered tools can help businesses optimise their listings for improved visibility and search rankings on the platform. These tools can analyse and update business information, such as hours of operation, services offered, and customer reviews, across all Google products, including Search and Maps. Additionally, AI can help businesses identify and correct any inconsistencies or errors in their Google My Business listings, ensuring that potential customers have accurate and up-to-date information.

Maintaining consistent and accurate business information across local listings is crucial for businesses targeting specific geographic areas, and AI-powered tools can help streamline this process. These tools can automatically scan and identify local business listings across various platforms and make updates to ensure consistent and accurate information, such as business name, address, phone number, and hours of operation. AI can also monitor and flag duplicate listings or inconsistent information across directories and help businesses resolve these issues promptly. By utilising AI-driven tools for local business listings management, businesses can ensure a positive customer experience and improve their local search visibility, ultimately driving more traffic and sales to their physical locations.

Link building is essential to any SEO strategy, and local link building is critical for businesses targeting specific geographic areas. AI can assist with identifying and prioritising local link-building opportunities. For example, AI-powered tools can analyse local backlinks from competitor sites and identify high-authority sites relevant to the business's industry and location. AI can also help identify broken links and suggest potential replacement links, ultimately improving the business's online presence and search engine ranking. By incorporating AI-driven link-building strategies, companies can gain a competitive advantage in local search results and increase their online visibility to potential customers in the area.

AI can assist with identifying potential local backlink opportunities by analysing data on a large scale. This includes identifying websites with high domain authority that are relevant to the business's industry and location, as well as analysing competitor backlink profiles to see which sites they have links from. AI can also help with outreach and building relationships with local websites and influencers for link-building purposes. By leveraging AI tools for local link building, businesses can improve their local search rankings and increase their visibility to potential customers in the area.

AI-driven tools can help businesses streamline and optimise their local link-building campaigns. For example, AI can assist with prospecting, outreach, and tracking results of link-building efforts. AI algorithms can analyse data on a large scale to identify potential link-building opportunities and sort them based on relevance and authority. AI can also assist with personalised outreach by analysing the contact information of potential link partners and providing suggestions for outreach strategies that are most likely to be successful. Additionally, AI can provide insights into the performance of link-building campaigns, allowing businesses to adjust their strategy accordingly for maximum effectiveness.

With the help of AI, it is possible to track and analyse local SEO performance in real time. AI-powered analytics tools can identify trends and patterns in data, such as search behaviour and user preferences, to help businesses refine their local SEO strategies. By analysing data from sources such as Google Analytics and Google Search Console, businesses can gain insights into their local search rankings, traffic, and engagement metrics. AI can also help identify areas for improvement and opportunities for growth in local search. By leveraging AI insights, businesses can continually optimise their local SEO strategies to drive more traffic and conversions.

Implementing AI-powered analytics tools for tracking local SEO performance can give businesses deep insights into their audience and how they interact with their website. With AI, companies can analyse a vast amount of data and identify patterns, trends, and opportunities to improve their local SEO strategies. AI-powered analytics tools can also help businesses track their local search rankings, traffic, and conversions and identify improvement areas. By leveraging AI for local SEO analytics, companies can gain a competitive edge and stay ahead of the curve in the ever-evolving local search landscape.

These tools provide real time data on website traffic, keyword rankings, and other relevant metrics. AI algorithms can analyse this data and provide actionable insights that can be used to improve local SEO strategies. For example, businesses can identify which local keywords drive the most traffic and adjust their content accordingly. They can also track the effectiveness of their local link-building efforts and adjust their campaigns as needed.

Mobile devices are increasingly becoming the primary means for searching for and accessing local businesses. As such, businesses must optimise their local SEO efforts for mobile devices. This is where AI can play a significant role. AI-powered tools can help businesses identify mobile-specific keywords and phrases and create optimised content for mobile devices. Additionally, AI can monitor mobile-specific search patterns and adjust local SEO strategies accordingly. By utilising AI for mobile local SEO optimisation, businesses can improve their visibility, attract more customers, and drive more sales.

With the increasing number of mobile device users, mobile optimisation has become crucial for local businesses to improve their search rankings. AI tools can help businesses understand how users interact with their websites on mobile devices, identify areas for improvement, and optimise their content for mobile viewing. Mobile optimisation involves making sites load faster, creating mobile-friendly content, and ensuring that contact information is easily accessible. AI can help businesses identify which mobile optimisations are most effective for improving local SEO, such as optimising for mobile keywords and creating content that is easily digestible on smaller screens.

AI can assist businesses in optimising their websites and content for mobile devices. AI-powered tools can analyse a website's mobile responsiveness, load speed, and user experience, among other factors, and provide insights and recommendations for improvement. This data can also be used to create mobile-specific content tailored to mobile users' unique needs and behaviours. By leveraging AI for mobile optimisation, businesses can improve their local SEO performance and ensure that they provide a seamless experience for users across all devices.

As the AI technology landscape continues to evolve, businesses must stay up-to-date on the latest advancements to remain competitive in local SEO. This includes staying informed about emerging AI technologies and their potential impact on local SEO, such as voice search, natural language processing, and machine learning. By keeping a finger on the pulse of AI developments, businesses can better prepare for the future of local SEO and stay ahead of the curve.

Adapting to changes in search engine algorithms and local user behaviour is crucial for long-term success in local SEO. As AI continues to evolve, it will likely play an increasingly important role in local search. Keeping up to date with the latest developments in AI and local search will be essential for businesses looking to stay ahead of the curve. Additionally, companies should consider investing in AI-driven tools and strategies to remain competitive in the local search landscape.

Integrating AI into long-term local SEO strategies involves understanding the evolving trends and changes in user behaviour and search engine algorithms. It also requires regular updating and refining strategies to take advantage of emerging AI technologies, such as machine learning and natural language processing, to optimise the local SEO performance. A long-term approach to local SEO incorporating AI can help businesses stay ahead of the competition and ensure that their online presence continues to attract and engage local customers.

Overall, AI is playing an increasingly important role in local SEO, offering businesses the ability to identify and target high-potential keywords, optimise content for local relevance, manage local business listings and streamline link-building campaigns, and track performance and adjust strategies accordingly. Additionally, the rise of voice search and mobile usage presents new challenges and opportunities for local SEO, which can be addressed by integrating AI technologies. By staying informed about emerging AI technologies and adapting to changes in search engine algorithms and user behaviour, businesses can leverage AI to gain a competitive edge and achieve long-term success in local SEO.

Incorporating AI into local SEO efforts can bring a range of benefits, such as increased efficiency, accuracy, and scalability. With AI-driven tools, businesses can streamline their local SEO processes and gain deeper insights into their performance. AI can also help companies to stay ahead of the curve in a rapidly evolving digital landscape by identifying and adapting to changes in search engine algorithms and user behaviour. Overall, embracing AI can help businesses to achieve greater visibility and success in local search results.

As AI technology continues to evolve, businesses that want to succeed in local SEO must adapt and embrace these advancements. By incorporating AI tools into their local SEO strategies, companies can gain a competitive edge by identifying high-potential local keywords, optimising their mobile devices and voice search content, managing local business listings, and improving local link building. Furthermore, AI-powered analytics can help businesses track their local SEO performance and extract valuable insights to inform future strategies. It is crucial for companies to stay informed about emerging AI technologies and their potential impact on local SEO and to integrate AI into their long-term local SEO strategies to remain competitive in an ever-evolving digital landscape.

To excel in local SEO, fostering a culture of innovation and adaptability is essential. This means staying up-to-date with the latest AI technologies and trends in the local SEO landscape and being willing to experiment and iterate with new strategies and tactics. It also means being open to feedback and insights generated by AI tools and using them to refine and improve your local SEO efforts continually. By embracing AI and prioritising innovation and adaptability, businesses can stay ahead of the competition and drive long-term success in local search.

Chapter Eleven: The Future

As we have embarked on exploring the future of AI and Google Search, it is essential to understand the role AI will play in shaping the digital landscape and identify the key trends and emerging technologies in AI-driven search and marketing. The advancements in AI have already transformed various aspects of our lives, and with continuous innovation, AI is poised to revolutionise how we interact with the digital world.

AI has the potential to significantly impact the digital landscape in numerous ways. By enabling a deeper understanding of user behaviour, AI-driven tools can provide more personalised, relevant, and timely information, making digital experiences increasingly seamless and efficient. Moreover, AI has the potential to transform the way businesses approach digital marketing, enabling them to harness the power of data for targeted and efficient campaigns. As AI continues to advance, we can expect it to play an even more critical role in shaping our digital experiences, affecting how we search, consume content, and engage with digital services.

As AI technologies continue to evolve, several key trends and emerging technologies are poised to define the future of AI-driven search and marketing. These include advancements in natural language understanding and generation, allowing search engines and digital marketing platforms to better understand and communicate with users. In addition, the integration of AI with emerging technologies such as augmented reality (AR) and virtual reality (VR) is expected to create immersive and interactive digital experiences that redefine the way users engage with search and marketing content.

As we delve deeper into this chapter, we will explore how these trends and emerging technologies are set to shape the future of AI-driven search and marketing. We will also discuss the potential challenges and opportunities that lie ahead, as well as the steps that organisations, policymakers, and individuals must take to ensure a responsible, ethical, and inclusive digital future.

The future of AI-driven search will be significantly influenced by advances in AI algorithms, which have the potential to improve search result relevance, personalisation, and user experience. In this section, we will discuss how improvements in search result relevance and personalisation, the evolution of natural language understanding and generation, and the integration of AI with emerging technologies such as AR and VR will shape the future of search.

As AI algorithms continue to evolve, they will become increasingly adept at understanding user intent, preferences, and context, leading to more relevant and personalised search results. This will result in a more tailored and engaging user experience, with search engines delivering precisely the information users seek. The ability to accurately predict user needs and deliver personalised content will also help search engines retain and attract users, fostering a competitive and innovative search ecosystem.

Advancements in natural language understanding (NLU) and natural language generation (NLG) will play a pivotal role in the future of AI-driven search. NLU enables search engines to better comprehend the context and meaning behind search queries, while NLG allows them to generate human-like responses and summaries. The combination of these two capabilities will not only improve the relevance and quality of search results but also facilitate more seamless and intuitive interactions between users and search engines. This will make searching for information more efficient and accessible, even for users with limited technical skills or language proficiency.

The integration of AI with emerging technologies like augmented reality (AR) and virtual reality (VR) is set to create new, immersive search experiences that blend the digital and physical worlds. Users will be able to interact with search results in novel ways, such as viewing 3D models or simulations, exploring virtual environments, or receiving context-aware information overlaid onto their physical surroundings. This will enable search engines to deliver richer, more engaging content that caters to diverse user needs and preferences. As AR and VR technologies become more prevalent and accessible, we can expect to see a growing convergence of AI-driven search and immersive digital experiences.

As AI continues to develop and reshape the digital landscape, it will also have a profound impact on the future of digital marketing. In this section, we will discuss the rise of intelligent automation and its implications for marketing efficiency, innovations in customer engagement through AI-generated content and interactions, and the shift towards data-driven, real time marketing strategies.

AI-driven intelligent automation is set to redefine digital marketing by automating a wide range of tasks, from content creation and ad targeting to campaign management and performance analysis. As AI algorithms become more sophisticated, they will be able to optimise marketing efforts in real time, allowing marketers to make data-driven decisions and allocate resources more efficiently. This will result in reduced costs, increased agility, and improved return on investment (ROI) for marketing campaigns. Furthermore, intelligent automation will free marketers from repetitive and mundane tasks, enabling them to focus on strategic initiatives and creative problem-solving.

AI-generated content and interactions will play a significant role in transforming customer engagement in the future of digital marketing. Chatbots, virtual assistants, and AI-driven personalisation engines will facilitate more dynamic and tailored customer interactions, helping brands establish deeper connections with their audiences. Furthermore, AI-generated content will enable marketers to produce more varied and compelling content at scale, enhancing the overall effectiveness of their campaigns. By leveraging AI-driven tools, marketers will be better equipped to create immersive and personalised experiences that resonate with diverse customer segments.

The future of digital marketing will be characterised by a shift towards data-driven, real time marketing strategies that harness the power of AI and big data analytics. By leveraging real time data and predictive analytics, marketers will be able to anticipate consumer needs, identify trends, and respond to market changes more rapidly. This will enable them to create more targeted and relevant marketing campaigns that drive engagement and conversion. In addition, real time marketing strategies will empower marketers to adapt and optimise campaigns on-the-fly, ensuring they remain relevant and effective in an ever-changing digital environment.

As AI continues to shape the digital landscape, it also has the potential to foster digital inclusivity and accessibility by bridging the digital divide and enhancing assistive technologies. In this section, we will discuss AI-driven tools that help bridge the digital divide, advancements in assistive technologies through AI, and the impact of AI on global information access and knowledge sharing.

AI-driven tools can play a crucial role in bridging the digital divide, which is the gap between those who have access to digital technologies and those who do not. By providing tailored educational resources, personalised learning experiences, and intuitive user interfaces, AI can help people from diverse backgrounds and with varying levels of digital literacy gain access to digital services and tools. AI-driven platforms can also break down language barriers, empowering users to communicate and access information in their native languages. By fostering digital inclusivity, AI can help ensure that everyone can benefit from the opportunities provided by the digital world.

AI advancements are poised to significantly enhance assistive technologies, making digital experiences more accessible to individuals with disabilities. For instance, AI-driven speech recognition and natural language processing can improve the functionality of voice-activated systems, enabling more seamless interactions for people with mobility impairments. Similarly, AI-powered image recognition and object detection can enhance the capabilities of screen readers and other visual aids, empowering individuals with visual impairments to navigate the digital world with greater ease. By leveraging AI to improve assistive technologies, we can create a more inclusive and accessible digital environment for all users.

AI has the potential to dramatically impact global information access and knowledge sharing by making it easier for users to find, process, and understand complex information. AI-driven search engines can surface relevant content from diverse sources, while AI-powered summarisation tools can distil lengthy documents into concise summaries, helping users quickly grasp key information. Additionally, AI-driven translation services can break down language barriers, enabling people from different linguistic backgrounds to access and share information more easily. By enhancing global information access and knowledge sharing, AI can play a vital role in fostering greater understanding and collaboration across cultural and geographic boundaries.

As AI continues to advance and permeate various aspects of our lives, it brings with it a host of ethical considerations and challenges that society must confront. In this section, we will discuss the future landscape of privacy, surveillance, and data ethics, address potential AI-driven social, economic, and cultural disparities, and consider the implications of autonomous decision-making and AI accountability.

The increasing integration of AI in our daily lives raises significant privacy, surveillance, and data ethics concerns. As AI systems become more sophisticated at processing and analysing personal information, the risk of intrusive data collection, unauthorised data sharing, and breaches of privacy grows. In addition, the potential for AI-driven surveillance and tracking technologies to erode personal autonomy and individual rights presents a significant challenge. As we navigate the future landscape of AI, it is crucial to establish strong privacy protections, promote transparency in data practices, and foster a culture of data ethics that upholds the rights and interests of individuals.

AI-driven systems and technologies have the potential to exacerbate social, economic, and cultural disparities if not carefully designed and implemented. Algorithmic biases can perpetuate existing inequalities, while the automation of jobs can disproportionately impact vulnerable populations. To mitigate these risks, we must ensure that AI systems are designed with fairness, inclusivity, and diversity in mind and that we implement policies and initiatives that address potential negative consequences, such as workforce retraining and social safety nets.

As AI systems become increasingly autonomous in their decision-making capabilities, it is crucial to consider the ethical implications of delegating critical decisions to machines. This raises questions about the appropriate balance between human oversight and machine autonomy, as well as the accountability of AI systems and their developers when things go wrong. To address these challenges, we must establish clear guidelines for AI-driven decision-making, develop frameworks for AI accountability, and foster an ongoing dialogue between stakeholders to navigate the complex ethical landscape surrounding autonomous AI systems.

The future of AI will not only be shaped by its own advancements but also by its intersection with other emerging technologies. In this section, we will explore how the convergence of AI with blockchain, the Internet of Things (IoT), and quantum computing will impact the digital landscape and present both opportunities and challenges for businesses, governments, and individuals.

The integration of AI with blockchain technology has the potential to create new opportunities for trust, security, and decentralisation in the digital landscape. Blockchain's distributed ledger system can enhance data security and transparency in AI systems, while AI can optimise blockchain processes and reduce computational requirements. The convergence of these technologies could lead to more secure and trustworthy AI-driven applications, such as decentralised and tamper-proof voting systems, supply chain management, and fraud detection.

The combination of AI and IoT technologies is set to transform the way we interact with the world around us. AI-driven IoT devices can analyse vast amounts of data in real time, enabling them to make autonomous decisions and optimise processes. This convergence has the potential to create smarter, more efficient, and interconnected systems across various sectors, such as smart cities, agriculture, transportation, and healthcare. However, the increasing reliance on interconnected systems also raises concerns about privacy, security, and the need for robust ethical guidelines to govern their development and implementation.

Quantum computing, with its potential to dramatically increase computational power, could have a significant impact on the future of AI. As quantum computers become more advanced, they will enable AI systems to solve complex problems and make predictions with unprecedented speed and accuracy. This could lead to breakthroughs in areas such as drug discovery, climate modelling, and cryptography. However, the intersection of AI and quantum computing also presents challenges, including the potential for AI-driven security threats and the need to balance the benefits of these powerful technologies with ethical considerations and societal implications.

As we continue to embrace AI and its transformative potential, it is crucial that we cultivate a sustainable and ethical AI-driven future that benefits all members of society. To ensure that individuals and communities can fully participate in and benefit from an AI-driven future, it is vital to promote digital literacy across all age groups and socioeconomic backgrounds. By equipping people with the necessary knowledge and skills to navigate the digital world, they can make informed decisions about the use and impact of AI-driven technologies in their lives. Digital literacy initiatives should also focus on teaching ethical values and responsible technology usage, encouraging individuals to engage with AI systems in a manner that aligns with their values and respects the rights of others.

Achieving a sustainable and ethical AI-driven future requires the collaboration and commitment of various stakeholders, including businesses, governments, academia, and civil society. By fostering open dialogue and partnerships, these stakeholders can work together to develop a shared vision of the AI future, addressing ethical concerns, anticipating potential risks, and identifying opportunities for positive impact. Collaborative efforts should also prioritise the development and implementation of inclusive AI policies and guidelines that safeguard human rights, promote fairness, and ensure accountability.

To cultivate a sustainable and ethical AI-driven future, it is essential for organisations to adopt responsible AI development and deployment practices. These practices should include diversity and inclusivity in AI research and development, the responsible collection and use of data, and the monitoring and mitigation of algorithmic biases and unintended consequences. Furthermore, organisations should prioritise transparency, accountability, and public engagement, ensuring that AI systems are designed and deployed in a manner that respects human rights, promotes trust, and supports long-term societal well-being. By adhering to responsible AI practices, businesses, governments, and other organisations can contribute to a more equitable and ethical AI-driven future.

While AI offers many potential benefits, it also brings with it risks that must be carefully managed. To effectively navigate the challenges of an AI-driven world, we must strike a balance between harnessing the positive aspects of AI and mitigating potential negative consequences. This requires ongoing evaluation and monitoring of AI systems, as well as the development of frameworks that support responsible AI development and deployment. By fostering a balanced approach, we can create a more resilient and adaptable AI-driven future.

As AI continues to evolve and disrupt traditional industries, lifelong learning and skills development will become increasingly important. Individuals will need to continually adapt to changes in the job market, acquiring new skills and knowledge to remain competitive and employable. To support this, educational institutions, businesses, and governments must collaborate to create flexible and accessible learning opportunities that empower individuals to take charge of their personal and professional development.

As AI systems become more sophisticated and pervasive, ethical considerations must play a central role in shaping AI policy and regulation. This involves identifying and addressing potential ethical concerns, such as privacy, fairness, accountability, and transparency, as well as fostering a culture of ethical AI development and deployment. Policymakers must work together with businesses, academia, and civil society to develop comprehensive regulatory frameworks that safeguard individual rights, promote public trust, and encourage innovation. By prioritising ethical considerations, we can ensure that AI-driven technologies are developed and implemented in a manner that respects human values and contributes to a more equitable and just future.

As we look towards an AI-driven future, it is essential to recognise that there will be unforeseen challenges and opportunities that emerge along the way. In this section, we will discuss the importance of building resilience and flexibility in our approach to AI, the need for proactive risk management, and fostering a culture of innovation and adaptability.

To navigate the unpredictable landscape of an AI-driven world, we must cultivate resilience and flexibility in our approach to AI. This means being open to change, learning from successes and failures, and adapting our strategies and practices as new information and insights become available. By fostering a resilient and flexible mindset, individuals, organisations, and societies will be better prepared to confront the challenges and harness the opportunities presented by AI.

As AI systems become more powerful and complex, the potential risks and unintended consequences also increase. Proactive risk management is crucial to minimise the potential negative impacts of AI technologies. This involves identifying and assessing potential risks, implementing safeguards and mitigation measures, and continuously monitoring and updating risk management strategies. By adopting a proactive approach to risk management, we can ensure that AI-driven technologies are developed and deployed in a responsible manner, reducing the likelihood of harmful consequences.

In an AI-driven world, innovation and adaptability are key to thriving in the face of change. Organisations, individuals, and societies must embrace a culture that encourages experimentation, learning, and continuous improvement. This involves investing in research and development, supporting cross-disciplinary collaboration, and fostering an environment that nurtures creative problem-solving and critical thinking. By embracing innovation and adaptability, we can harness the full potential of AI-driven technologies and create a more resilient and sustainable future.

Chapter Twelve: Navigating the Ethical Concerns

As the world becomes increasingly digitalised, the role of artificial intelligence (AI) and its influence on our daily lives cannot be overstated. In particular, Google Search, a key player in the AI and digital ecosystem, has transformed how we access, process, and utilise information. As AI and Google Search continue to grow in power and reach, it is vital to address the ethical concerns that emerge from their intersection.

AI and machine learning have experienced rapid growth and development over the past decade. As a result, AI-powered systems have become deeply integrated into various aspects of our lives, shaping our digital experiences and facilitating a myriad of tasks that were once time-consuming or labour-intensive.

Google Search stands as a prominent example of AI integration, having transformed the way we locate and process information. In a world inundated with data, Google's AI algorithms filter through vast amounts of information to provide users with relevant and accurate search results, making the web a more navigable space for billions of people.

However, the increasing reliance on AI and Google Search also brings forth a range of ethical concerns that need to be carefully considered. The sheer power and influence of these technologies, and their potential to shape human behaviour and thought, demand that we develop a deep understanding of the ethical implications that emerge from their widespread use.

Given the pervasive nature of AI and Google Search, it is crucial to address the ethical concerns that arise from their application. As these technologies become further embedded into the fabric of our society, the need for a careful examination of their ethical dimensions only grows more urgent.

As we continue to explore the intersections of AI, Google Search, and ethical considerations, the following sections will delve into the specific concerns surrounding these technologies, as well as potential strategies for navigating and mitigating the ethical challenges they pose. It is our collective responsibility to ensure that the technological advancements of the digital era remain firmly grounded in ethical principles and considerations, ultimately fostering a more just and equitable society.

As AI-driven Google Search continues to shape the digital landscape, it is essential to delve into the ethical concerns associated with its widespread use. In this section, we will examine the potential for algorithmic bias in AI-enhanced search results, privacy and data protection issues, and the implications of AI-generated content and deep fakes on the credibility of search results.

At the heart of Google Search lies sophisticated AI algorithms that analyse, rank, and present information based on relevance, quality, and user preferences. However, the very nature of these algorithms can give rise to unintentional biases, which are often rooted in the data used to train the AI models. These biases can manifest in several ways, such as over-representing specific perspectives, reinforcing stereotypes, or inadvertently marginalising certain groups.

It is crucial to recognise and address these biases in AI-enhanced search results, as they can have far-reaching consequences on the perception of truth and fairness in the digital realm. To mitigate these biases, stakeholders should focus on diversifying data sets, refining algorithms, and employing diverse teams that can better identify and address potential issues. Additionally, promoting transparency in AI decision-making processes can help build trust and ensure that search engines are held accountable for the information they present.

The increasing reliance on AI-driven search engines has raised concerns about privacy and data protection. To provide personalised search results, AI algorithms rely on vast amounts of data collected from users, including their search history, location, and browsing habits. This raises questions about the extent to which users' privacy is being compromised and whether the information collected is adequately safeguarded against potential misuse.

To navigate this ethical challenge, it is essential to develop robust privacy policies and practices that respect users' rights and expectations. This includes transparent disclosure of data collection methods, adherence to data protection regulations, and the implementation of strong security measures to protect against data breaches. Furthermore, giving users more control over their data and the ability to manage their privacy settings can empower individuals to make informed decisions about their digital footprint.

The rise of AI-generated content and deep fakes poses a significant threat to the credibility of search results. Advanced AI technologies have made it increasingly possible to create realistic yet falsified content such as images, videos, and text. The presence of this misleading content in search results can undermine trust in the information found online and potentially spread disinformation.

To combat the impact of AI-generated content and deep fakes on search results, it is important to develop AI-driven solutions capable of identifying and flagging such content. Additionally, fostering collaborations between search engines, content creators, and platforms can help establish guidelines and standards to minimise the spread of deceptive content. Education initiatives that promote digital literacy can also empower users to recognise and critically evaluate the credibility of information found online.

As we grapple with the ethical concerns arising from AI-driven Google Search, it is vital to continuously reassess and refine our approaches to ensure that the benefits of these technologies are maximised while mitigating their potential harm. Only through thoughtful consideration and responsible action can we harness the true potential of AI to shape the digital landscape positively.

The rapid advancement of AI technologies has led to a transformation in digital marketing practices. While these developments have unlocked new opportunities for marketers, they have also given rise to ethical concerns that warrant careful consideration. In this section, we will explore targeting and personalisation issues, ethical considerations in the use of AI-generated content and customer interactions, and transparency and accountability challenges in AI-driven marketing campaigns.

AI-driven digital marketing enables the delivery of highly targeted and personalised advertisements based on users' behaviour, preferences, and demographics. While this can lead to a more relevant and engaging user experience, it also raises ethical concerns regarding intrusive advertising and the potential erosion of privacy. Ads that are overly personalised or invasive can create discomfort for users and may exploit vulnerable individuals, such as those struggling with addiction or mental health issues.

To address these concerns, it is essential to establish ethical guidelines for the degree of targeting and personalisation employed in digital marketing campaigns.

This may involve setting limits on the data collected and used for targeting, as well as providing users with the option to opt out of personalised advertising or manage their privacy settings. By striking a balance between effective marketing and respecting users' boundaries, marketers can build trust and foster positive relationships with their audience.

AI-generated content and customer interactions, such as chatbots and virtual assistants, are increasingly being utilised in digital marketing to enhance customer experiences and streamline processes. However, the use of these AI-driven technologies raises ethical questions related to transparency, deception, and the potential manipulation of user emotions or decision-making.

To navigate these ethical considerations, marketers should be transparent about the use of AI-generated content and interactions, clearly disclosing their nature and purpose to users. Additionally, AI-driven technologies should be designed with the user's best interests in mind, avoiding manipulative tactics or the exploitation of vulnerabilities. By prioritising ethical design and transparent practices, marketers can leverage AI-generated content and interactions in a way that respects users and fosters positive experiences.

AI-driven marketing campaigns often involve complex algorithms and data processing techniques, which can make it challenging for users and regulators to understand how decisions are being made. This lack of transparency can hinder accountability and raise concerns over fairness, bias, and potential misuse of user data.

To address transparency and accountability challenges, marketers should strive to provide clear and accessible explanations of their AI-driven processes and algorithms. Where possible, open and collaborative communication with users, regulators, and other stakeholders can help build trust and ensure that AI-driven marketing campaigns adhere to ethical standards. Furthermore, the implementation of external audits or third-party oversight can bolster accountability and promote best practices within the industry.

In order to navigate the ethical concerns surrounding AI and Google Search integration, it is imperative to establish ethical guidelines that can guide the development and application of these technologies. In this section, we will discuss the importance of developing clear ethical principles for AI-driven search and marketing practices, incorporating fairness, accountability, and transparency into AI algorithms and applications, and encouraging industry-wide adoption of ethical guidelines and best practices.

Creating a set of clear ethical principles is a critical step in ensuring that AI-driven search and marketing practices adhere to the highest standards of integrity and responsibility. These principles should be grounded in a commitment to respect user rights, prioritise fairness, maintain transparency, and promote accountability in the development and deployment of AI technologies. By establishing a shared ethical foundation, stakeholders can work together to address potential challenges and create a digital ecosystem that benefits all parties involved.

The integration of fairness, accountability, and transparency into AI algorithms and applications is essential to addressing the ethical concerns that emerge from AI and Google Search integration. This involves the rigorous examination of AI models and data sets for potential biases, as well as the development of techniques to mitigate any identified issues. Ensuring accountability requires the establishment of mechanisms for monitoring, reporting, and addressing potential ethical lapses in AI-driven technologies. Lastly, fostering transparency involves

the clear communication of AI processes and decision-making to users, regulators, and other stakeholders.
The widespread adoption of ethical guidelines and best practices across the industry is crucial for fostering a responsible digital ecosystem. This requires collaboration between businesses, regulators, and academia to share knowledge, develop industry standards, and promote responsible AI practices. By creating a culture of ethical commitment and continuous improvement, the industry can ensure that AI-driven search and marketing technologies contribute positively to society while minimising potential harm.

As AI continues to shape the digital landscape, it is essential to focus on the ethical development and deployment of AI technologies. This encompasses ensuring diversity and inclusivity in AI development teams and processes, implementing responsible data collection, storage, and usage practices, and monitoring AI-driven tools for unintended consequences and biases.

Diversity and inclusivity play a critical role in mitigating the risks of bias and fostering the development of ethical AI technologies. By ensuring that AI development teams are diverse in terms of background, expertise, and perspectives, organisations can create more robust and unbiased AI models. Inclusivity in the development process also involves engaging with various stakeholders, including users and marginalised communities, to understand their needs and concerns. By prioritising diversity and inclusivity, organisations can develop AI technologies that are more ethically sound and better serve a broader range of users.

Data is the lifeblood of AI-driven technologies, and responsible data management is fundamental to the ethical development and deployment of AI tools. Organisations should develop clear policies and guidelines around data collection, storage, and usage to ensure compliance with data protection regulations and respect for user privacy. This may involve adopting privacy-enhancing techniques such as anonymisation, implementing strong security measures to prevent data breaches, and giving users more control over their personal data. By upholding responsible data management practices, organisations can build trust with users and support the ethical development of AI technologies.

AI-driven tools can sometimes exhibit unintended consequences or biases due to the complexity of their underlying algorithms or the data used to train them. It is essential to establish mechanisms for monitoring and evaluating AI tools for potential issues, as well as refining and adjusting them when necessary. This involves conducting regular audits and assessments of AI models, staying up-to-date with the latest research on bias detection and mitigation techniques, and being receptive to user feedback. By actively monitoring AI-driven tools for unintended consequences and biases, organisations can foster a culture of continuous improvement and ensure the ethical deployment of AI technologies.

Organisations must navigate the complex legal and regulatory frameworks governing their development and deployment. This involves understanding the evolving landscape of AI-related laws and regulations, complying with data protection and privacy laws, and collaborating with policymakers and industry leaders to shape future regulations.

The legal landscape surrounding AI technologies is constantly evolving as policymakers grapple with the ethical, social, and economic implications of these advancements. Organisations must stay abreast of the latest developments in AI-related laws and regulations, which may include provisions on algorithmic transparency, fairness, liability, and intellectual property rights. This requires continuous monitoring of regulatory changes, as well as investing in resources to ensure compliance with all relevant laws and regulations, both domestically and internationally.

Data protection and privacy laws, such as the General Data Protection Regulation (GDPR) in the European Union and the California Consumer Privacy Act (CCPA) in the United States, have significant implications for organisations utilising AI-driven technologies. These regulations often impose stringent requirements on data collection, storage, usage, and sharing, as well as granting users specific rights concerning their personal data. Organisations must develop and maintain robust compliance programs to ensure adherence to these laws, which may include appointing dedicated data protection officers, conducting privacy impact assessments, and providing transparent information about data processing activities to users.

As AI-related laws and regulations continue to evolve, it is crucial for organisations to actively engage with policymakers and industry leaders to shape future regulatory frameworks. This collaborative approach can help to ensure that future regulations are informed by the latest technological advancements and industry insights while addressing the ethical, social, and economic concerns arising from AI technologies. By participating in industry associations, standard-setting organisations, and policy forums, organisations can contribute to the development of balanced regulatory frameworks that support innovation and protect the interests of all stakeholders.

Educating stakeholders about ethical AI and Google Search practices is vital for fostering a culture of responsibility and accountability within the industry. This involves raising awareness among employees, customers, and partners about ethical concerns, providing training and resources to help stakeholders make informed decisions, and encouraging open dialogue and collaboration to address ethical challenges.

Creating awareness among stakeholders is the first step in ensuring that ethical concerns are taken into account in the development and deployment of AI-driven technologies. Organisations should prioritise communicating the ethical implications of AI and Google Search practices to employees, customers, and partners, emphasising the importance of responsible AI usage. This can be achieved through regular updates, workshops, seminars, and other awareness-raising initiatives.

Once stakeholders are aware of the ethical concerns surrounding AI and Google Search practices, it is crucial to equip them with the knowledge and tools necessary to make informed decisions. This may involve providing targeted training programs, resources, and guidance for different stakeholder groups, such as developers, marketers, or executives. For example, developers can be trained in bias detection and mitigation techniques, while marketers can learn about responsible data collection and targeting practices. By offering comprehensive training and resources, organisations can empower stakeholders to contribute to the ethical development and use of AI-driven technologies.

Encouraging open dialogue and collaboration among stakeholders is key to addressing the ethical challenges associated with AI and Google Search practices. By fostering a culture of open communication and collaboration, organisations can create an environment where stakeholders can voice their concerns, share their expertise, and work together to develop solutions that address ethical issues. This may involve establishing dedicated forums or channels for discussing ethical matters, hosting regular roundtables or workshops to explore specific concerns, or partnering with external organisations and experts to gain additional insights.

The ethical application of AI in the context of Google Search and digital marketing can significantly contribute to building trust with consumers and enhancing customer experiences. In this section, we will explore how ethical AI practices can strengthen consumer trust and brand reputation, as well as the potential for ethical AI to drive more meaningful and personalised customer experiences.

As consumers become increasingly aware of the ethical concerns surrounding AI technologies, organisations that prioritise and implement ethical AI practices can differentiate themselves and build stronger consumer trust. By adhering to ethical guidelines, organisations demonstrate a commitment to user rights, fairness, transparency, and accountability, which can, in turn, enhance their brand reputation. Consumers are more likely to trust and engage with brands that are transparent about their AI practices, respect user privacy, and actively work to mitigate potential harms associated with AI-driven technologies. In this way, ethical AI practices not only contribute to consumer trust but also create long-term value for organisations.

Ethical AI practices can also play a critical role in delivering more meaningful and personalised customer experiences. By prioritising fairness and transparency, organisations can develop AI-driven tools that better understand and cater to the diverse needs and preferences of their users. This can lead to more relevant search results, personalised recommendations, and targeted marketing campaigns that resonate with users and build lasting connections.

Moreover, ethical AI practices can help organisations address privacy concerns by implementing responsible data collection and usage practices. By providing users with control over their personal data and ensuring that data is used ethically and transparently, organisations can create personalised experiences that respect user privacy and maintain trust.

As AI continues to advance and its integration with Google Search and digital marketing becomes more sophisticated, organisations must prepare for the future of ethical AI. This involves staying informed about emerging ethical concerns and potential solutions, adapting to changes in technology, user behaviour, and regulatory environments, and developing a proactive approach to ethical challenges in AI and search engine marketing.

To stay ahead of the curve, organisations must continually monitor and engage with the latest research, industry developments, and best practices related to ethical AI and Google Search. This involves staying informed about emerging ethical concerns, potential solutions, and new technologies that may impact AI-driven search and marketing practices. By participating in industry events, engaging with expert communities, and closely following the latest news and academic research, organisations can ensure they are prepared to address new ethical challenges as they arise.

The rapid pace of technological advancement, shifting user behaviour, and evolving regulatory environments necessitate organisations to be agile and adaptive in their approach to ethical AI and Google Search. This may involve periodically reassessing and updating their ethical principles, policies, and practices in response to new developments or stakeholder expectations. Additionally, organisations must be prepared to adapt their AI-driven tools and algorithms to maintain compliance with changing legal and regulatory requirements, as well as to meet the evolving needs of their users.

A proactive approach to ethical challenges in AI and search engine marketing is essential for organisations looking to thrive in the future digital landscape. This requires anticipating potential ethical issues before they arise and taking steps to mitigate them. Organisations should invest in ongoing education, training, and resources to ensure their teams are equipped with the knowledge and skills necessary to identify and address ethical concerns. Furthermore, they should foster a culture of ethical responsibility, where stakeholders are encouraged to actively consider and engage with ethical issues in their day-to-day work.

As we conclude our exploration of the ethical concerns surrounding AI-driven search and marketing practices, it becomes increasingly clear that embracing ethical AI is paramount for building a sustainable digital future. In this final section, we will reiterate the importance of prioritising ethical considerations in AI-driven search and marketing practices, the role of businesses, policymakers, and individuals in shaping a responsible digital landscape, and the potential for ethical AI to drive positive change and create a more equitable online ecosystem.

The integration of AI into search and marketing practices has unlocked unprecedented opportunities for growth, efficiency, and personalisation. However, it has also introduced complex ethical concerns that must be addressed to ensure a responsible digital future. By prioritising ethical considerations, organisations can mitigate potential harms, build consumer trust, and create more inclusive, equitable, and meaningful experiences for users. Embracing ethical AI practices is not only the right thing to do, but it also contributes to long-term value and sustainability for businesses.

Creating a responsible digital landscape requires the concerted efforts of all stakeholders, including businesses, policymakers, and individuals. Businesses must commit to responsible AI development and deployment, adhere to ethical guidelines, and engage in ongoing education and dialogue around ethical concerns. Policymakers must establish clear regulatory frameworks that balance innovation with protection for users and society. Finally, individuals must be informed and engaged in the conversation around ethical AI, advocating for their rights and holding organisations accountable.

When applied ethically, AI-driven technologies hold the potential to drive positive change and create a more equitable online ecosystem. Ethical AI practices can help dismantle systemic biases, foster transparency, and promote fairness in digital experiences. Moreover, ethical AI can contribute to more personalised, user-centric experiences that respect privacy and build meaningful connections between organisations and their audiences. By embracing ethical AI, stakeholders across the digital landscape can contribute to a sustainable, equitable, and inclusive digital future for all.

Chapter Thirteen: Conclusion Harnessing the Power of AI

As we conclude this comprehensive exploration of AI, Google Search, and digital marketing, it is vital to reflect on the insights and knowledge gained throughout this book. We have delved into the foundational concepts and intricacies of AI, its integration with Google Search, and the vast potential of AI-driven digital marketing strategies. Along the way, we have also tackled the ethical concerns and challenges that arise from these cutting-edge technologies and their impact on society. Now, it is time to acknowledge the transformative potential of AI in the digital marketing landscape and consider the role each one of us plays in harnessing its power for the greater good.

Throughout this book, we have explored the many facets of AI and its applications in the realm of Google Search and digital marketing. We have gained insights into how AI algorithms can revolutionise the way users find and consume information, as well as how businesses can leverage these advanced technologies to enhance their marketing efforts. We have examined the power of AI-driven tools such as chatbots, recommendation engines, and content generation software and their potential to elevate the user experience, improve engagement, and drive business growth. Furthermore, we have delved into the ethical and legal implications of using AI-driven systems, stressing the importance of addressing these concerns as we continue to innovate and adapt to the rapidly evolving digital landscape.

As we have seen throughout this book, AI holds immense potential to reshape the digital marketing landscape in ways that were previously unimaginable. With its ability to process vast amounts of data, analyse complex patterns, and learn from experience, AI is set to revolutionise the way businesses target and interact with their customers, offering more personalised and relevant experiences. The seamless integration of AI with Google Search and other digital marketing channels will enable organisations to develop more efficient and effective strategies that drive measurable results and long-term success. However, it is also crucial to recognise the potential risks and challenges associated with the rapid adoption of AI and to ensure that we develop and implement these technologies in a responsible, ethical, and sustainable manner. As we embrace the transformative power of AI, we must strive to harness its potential for the benefit of all stakeholders, including businesses, consumers, and society as a whole.

As we navigate the increasingly complex and competitive digital landscape, it is crucial to recognise the synergy between AI and Google Search and the opportunities this powerful combination presents. By leveraging the capabilities of AI technologies in digital marketing strategies, businesses can maximise their potential for growth and success, and create meaningful and personalised experiences for their customers.

In today's fast-paced digital world, businesses need to stay agile and adaptive to remain competitive. This is where the power of AI-driven technologies comes into play, enabling organisations to derive insights from vast amounts of data, optimise their marketing campaigns, and deliver more relevant and engaging content. By integrating AI technologies into digital marketing strategies, businesses can achieve greater efficiency, effectiveness, and responsiveness, ultimately driving stronger results and higher returns on investment. As we have explored throughout this book, AI-driven tools such as chatbots, personalisation engines, and content generation software offer significant advantages in terms of customer engagement, targeting, and overall marketing performance. Thus, leveraging AI technologies should be a key priority for businesses looking to stay ahead in the digital marketing landscape.

The integration of AI into Google Search has been transformative, offering users faster, more accurate, and more personalised search results. By harnessing the power of AI, Google Search has evolved into a highly sophisticated tool that can understand complex queries, decipher user intent, and deliver relevant and useful information in real time. For businesses, this offers unprecedented opportunities to connect with their target audience, understand their needs and preferences, and provide tailored solutions that drive engagement and conversions. By embracing the synergy between AI and Google Search, organisations can optimise their search engine optimisation (SEO) strategies, enhance their visibility in search results, and ensure they are providing the most valuable and relevant content to their users. By doing so, they can maximise the potential of this powerful combination and stay ahead in the ever-changing digital marketing landscape.

As the impact of AI-driven technologies continues to grow, it is essential for businesses to adapt and prepare for the AI revolution. This involves adjusting organisational structures and processes, investing in AI education and training for employees, and cultivating a culture of innovation and continuous learning.

In order to successfully integrate AI-driven technologies into their operations, businesses must be willing to adapt their organisational structures and processes. This may involve reevaluating traditional roles and hierarchies, streamlining decision-making processes, and encouraging cross-functional collaboration. By creating an agile and flexible organisational environment, businesses can more effectively incorporate AI-driven technologies and harness their potential to drive growth and success.

As AI becomes an increasingly important component of the business landscape, it is vital for companies to invest in AI education and training for their employees. This ensures that team members have the knowledge and skills required to effectively work with AI-driven tools and technologies and can fully leverage the benefits they offer. By providing employees with ongoing education and training opportunities, businesses can foster a workforce that is prepared to adapt and thrive in the face of AI-driven change.

In order to fully harness the potential of AI and remain competitive in the rapidly evolving digital landscape, businesses must cultivate a culture of innovation and continuous learning. This involves encouraging employees to embrace new ideas, take risks, and learn from both successes and failures. By fostering an environment that values innovation, creativity, and continuous improvement, businesses can stay at the forefront of AI-driven developments and ensure they are well-positioned to capitalise on emerging opportunities. As we embrace the AI revolution, it is crucial for businesses to prioritise adaptability, education, and innovation in order to harness the full potential of AI-driven technologies and drive long-term success.

The rapid advancement of AI technologies requires a collective effort among various stakeholders to ensure success and drive sustainable innovation. In this context, embracing collaboration through partnerships with technology providers, AI experts, and digital marketing agencies is crucial. Moreover, fostering a culture of collaboration and knowledge-sharing among industry stakeholders and building strong networks to facilitate AI adoption and innovation are essential steps towards realising the full potential of AI.

One of the most effective ways for businesses to harness the power of AI is by partnering with technology providers, AI experts, and digital marketing agencies. These collaborations offer access to valuable resources, knowledge, and cutting-edge technologies that can help businesses stay ahead of the curve in the ever-changing digital landscape. By working together, organisations can develop and implement AI-driven solutions that are tailored to their specific needs and objectives, ultimately driving better results and long-term success.

To ensure the responsible development and deployment of AI technologies, it is important for businesses to encourage collaboration and knowledge-sharing among industry stakeholders. By fostering open dialogue and cooperation, organisations can pool their resources, share best practices, and collectively address the challenges and opportunities presented by AI. Such collaboration can also facilitate the development of industry-wide standards and guidelines, promoting ethical and responsible AI practices that benefit businesses, consumers, and society as a whole.

In order to maximise the potential of AI, businesses should focus on building strong networks that facilitate AI adoption and innovation. This involves connecting with other businesses, research institutions, government agencies, and non-profit organisations that share a common interest in AI and its potential applications. By establishing these networks, businesses can tap into a wealth of knowledge, resources, and expertise, driving innovation and enabling more efficient and effective AI-driven solutions. By embracing collaboration and fostering strong partnerships, businesses can fully harness the power of AI, ensuring a sustainable and successful future in the rapidly evolving digital landscape.

As businesses and individuals alike embrace the transformative power of AI, it is important to address the challenges that come with the adoption of these technologies. This involves tackling ethical concerns, data privacy, and regulatory compliance, as well as preparing for potential risks and challenges associated with AI technologies. Ultimately, the key to success in the future of AI lies in staying agile and adaptive to the rapidly evolving landscape.

One of the most pressing issues surrounding AI adoption is the need to address ethical concerns, data privacy, and regulatory compliance. As AI technologies become more prevalent, businesses must take responsibility for ensuring that their practices are ethically sound, protect user privacy, and adhere to relevant laws and regulations. This requires a proactive approach to understanding and addressing these challenges, including the development of robust ethical frameworks, the implementation of privacy-enhancing technologies, and the establishment of open dialogue with regulators and policymakers.

As businesses adopt AI technologies, they must also be prepared to face potential risks and challenges. This includes addressing the possibilities of algorithmic bias, security vulnerabilities, and unintended consequences that may arise from the use of AI-driven tools. To effectively mitigate these risks, businesses should adopt a comprehensive risk management approach, continuously monitor the performance and impact of their AI systems, and actively seek to identify and address any issues that may arise.

The AI landscape is rapidly evolving, with new advancements and applications emerging on a regular basis. To stay ahead of the curve and fully harness the potential of AI, businesses must remain agile and adaptive to these changes. This includes staying informed about the latest developments in AI technologies, regularly reassessing their strategies and processes, and fostering a culture of innovation and continuous learning. By remaining adaptable and responsive, businesses can seize emerging opportunities, overcome challenges, and confidently navigate the future of AI.

The increasing adoption of AI technologies in digital marketing and other sectors presents both opportunities and challenges. It is essential for businesses to strike a balance between profitability and responsibility, ensuring the responsible use of AI technologies while striving for sustainable growth. This involves fostering a commitment to environmental and social sustainability, which is key to long-term success.

As businesses adopt AI technologies in digital marketing and other areas, they must prioritise responsible use. This includes being transparent about the use of AI-driven tools, adhering to ethical principles, and working to minimise negative impacts on consumers and society at large. By embracing responsible AI practices, businesses can build trust with their customers, enhance their brand reputation, and contribute positively to the digital landscape.

Balancing business growth and ethical considerations is crucial for sustainable success. While the pursuit of profitability is essential, it should not come at the expense of ethical standards and social responsibility. Businesses should actively seek to identify and address potential ethical concerns, such as algorithmic bias, data privacy, and the impact of AI on job displacement. By fostering a culture of ethical awareness and decision-making, organisations can ensure that they achieve growth while maintaining their commitment to responsible business practices.

In addition to balancing profitability and responsibility, businesses must also prioritise environmental and social sustainability in their AI-driven endeavours. This involves considering the environmental footprint of AI technologies, such as the energy consumption associated with large-scale data processing, and working to minimise these impacts. It also includes supporting social sustainability by investing in education, workforce development, and equitable access to AI-driven technologies. By demonstrating a commitment to environmental and social sustainability, businesses can build a strong foundation for long-term success and contribute to a better future for all.

As we look towards the future of AI-driven digital marketing, it is important to explore the potential impact of AI on the industry and anticipate breakthroughs, innovations, and trends that will shape the marketing ecosystem. By understanding the potential developments in AI-driven marketing, businesses can better prepare for the changes ahead and position themselves for success.

The integration of AI into digital marketing is already driving significant changes across the industry. As AI continues to advance, we can expect even more profound impacts on the future of marketing. AI-powered tools and platforms will likely become more sophisticated and accessible, enabling businesses to create highly personalised, targeted campaigns that deliver improved ROI. Additionally, AI will likely play an increasing role in automating and streamlining various marketing tasks, from content creation to data analysis, allowing marketers to focus on more strategic initiatives.

Furthermore, AI-driven insights may revolutionise the way marketers understand and engage with their customers, fostering the development of more impactful, emotionally resonant campaigns. AI will likely also play a crucial role in improving the overall customer experience as businesses leverage AI-powered tools to create seamless, personalised interactions across multiple channels.

As AI continues to develop, we can expect to see numerous breakthroughs, innovations, and trends that will shape the marketing ecosystem. One such trend is the rise of voice search and AI-driven conversational agents, which will likely change the way consumers search for and interact with brands. As voice-based technologies become more prevalent, businesses will need to adapt their strategies to ensure they remain visible and relevant in this new landscape.

Another anticipated innovation is the growing use of AI in content generation, with tools becoming increasingly sophisticated at producing human-like text, images, and even video content. This has the potential to revolutionise content marketing by enabling businesses to create highly customised, contextually relevant content at scale.

Furthermore, advances in AI-driven analytics will likely provide marketers with deeper, more actionable insights into customer behaviour, preferences, and sentiment. This data will enable marketers to create more targeted, effective campaigns and make more informed strategic decisions.

As we conclude this exploration of AI, Google Search, and digital marketing, it is our hope that the insights, knowledge, and examples presented throughout the book have inspired readers to harness the potential of AI in their digital marketing endeavours. By adopting a forward-thinking mindset and embracing change, businesses and individuals alike can play a pivotal role in transforming the digital marketing landscape and creating a more efficient, personalised, and connected world.

We encourage readers to take the lessons and best practices gleaned from this book and apply them to their own digital marketing strategies. By embracing the power of AI-driven technologies, businesses can improve customer experiences, create more effective campaigns, and drive sustainable growth. This not only benefits the individual organisation but also contributes to a more vibrant and competitive digital ecosystem where businesses of all sizes and industries can flourish.

To fully harness the potential of AI, it is essential for businesses and individuals to adopt a forward-thinking mindset and embrace change. This involves staying informed about the latest AI advancements, experimenting with new technologies, and learning from both successes and failures. By fostering a culture of innovation, curiosity, and continuous learning, organisations can navigate the rapidly evolving digital landscape and seize emerging opportunities.

We firmly believe in the power of AI to transform the digital marketing landscape and create a more efficient, personalised, and connected world. By leveraging the capabilities of AI-driven technologies, businesses can enhance their marketing strategies, better understand and serve their customers, and drive sustainable growth. As we continue to explore and harness the potential of AI, the future of digital marketing promises to be more dynamic, innovative, and exciting than ever before.

Printed in Great Britain
by Amazon

24469483R00096